James William Redhouse, Shah of Persia

A Summarized Translation with Verbatim Extracts of the Diary of

H.M. the Shah of Persia

During his Tour through Europe in A.D. 1873

James William Redhouse, Shah of Persia

A Summarized Translation with Verbatim Extracts of the Diary of H.M. the Shah of Persia
During his Tour through Europe in A.D. 1873

ISBN/EAN: 9783337124441

Printed in Europe, USA, Canada, Australia, Japan

Cover: Foto ©ninafisch / pixelio.de

More available books at **www.hansebooks.com**

By Her Majesty's Command.

A SUMMARIZED TRANSLATION,

WITH

VERBATIM EXTRACTS,

OF THE

DIARY

OF

H. M. THE SHAH OF PERSIA,

DURING HIS

TOUR THROUGH EUROPE IN A.D. 1873.

BY

J. W. REDHOUSE, Esq.,
ORIENTAL TRANSLATOR, FOREIGN OFFICE.

London:
HARRISON AND SONS, ST. MARTIN'S LANE,
Printers in Ordinary to Her Majesty.

1874.

TABLE OF CONTENTS.

	Page
Leave Tehran for Enzeli, on the Caspian	1
Arrive at Astrakhan	2
Reach Moscow and St. Petersburg	5
Leave St. Petersburg for Berlin	9
Arrive at Berlin	11
Leave Berlin; visit M. Krupp's works, and arrive at Cologne	17
Ascend the Rhine to Wiesbaden	18
Visit Schierstein, Biebrich, and Frankfort	19
Visit Darmstadt and Baden-Baden	21
Descend the Rhine and proceed to Spa	23
At Spa	24
Arrive at Brussels	27
Embark at Ostend for England	29
Reach Dover	31
Arrive in London; visit the Prince of Wales, Duke of Edinburgh, &c.	34
Dine with the Prince of Wales; party at Stafford House	39
First visit to Windsor Castle; receive the Order of the Garter	40
Visit to the Guildhall	45
Visit Woolwich	49
The Opera	51
The Zoological Gardens	52
Excursion to Portsmouth for the Naval Review	54
First visit to the Albert Hall	58
Review of troops in Windsor Park	61
Visit to the Docks and Greenwich by water	65
Excursion to Liverpool, Trentham Hall, and Manchester	70
Visit to Chiswick	79
Visit to Richmond and Earl Russell	82
First visit to the Crystal Palace	86
Visits to the Tower, St. Paul's, and the Bank	91
To the Houses of Parliament and Westminster Abbey	93
Visit of adieu to Her Majesty at Windsor	97

	Page
Madame Tussaud's Exhibition	100
Second visit to the Crystal Palace	102
Second visit to the Albert Hall	106
Visit St. Thomas's Hospital	108
Visit the Duke of Argyll	109
The Albert Memorial; Drury Lane Theatre	110
Leave London, viâ Portsmouth, for France	112
Arrive at Cherbourg and Paris	113
Leave Paris, viâ Dijon, for Geneva	136
Arrive at Turin, viâ Mont Cenis tunnel	143
Arrive at Milan	147
Leave Milan for Saltzburg, viâ Verona	149
Arrive at Laxenburg, Vienna	152
Leave Vienna, viâ Saltzburg, &c., for Brindisi	162
Leave Brindisi	169
Arrive at Constantinople	172
Leave Constantinople for Poti and Tiflis	184
Leave Tiflis for Baku	191
Leave Baku	194
Overtaken by a storm	195
Land at Enzeli	198

DIARY OF H.M. THE SHAH OF PERSIA

DURING HIS TOUR THROUGH EUROPE

IN

A.D. 1873.

ON Saturday, the 19th April, 1873, we started on our tour in Europe, spending a few days in the neighbourhood of the capital, and arriving at Resht on the 10th of May, after suffering severely from heavy rains, cold winds, and even frost, in the mountainous district through which part of our road lay. Prince Menschikoff, sent from St. Petersburg to attend upon us, met us outside this town; the day following we embarked on board a small steamer, recently purchased and fitted up by our command, and, accompanied by two other similar vessels belonging to the Russian navy, we proceeded to Enzeli, and the next day, the 12th of May, were received on board the "Constantine," and left for Astrakhan, accompanied a short distance by several Russian men-of-war steamers. Next morning, being off Baku, we sent some messages on shore to be telegraphed to Tehran and to Europe. We arrived off the mouth of the Volga, and were transhipped to a river-boat towed by a steamer, in which we reached Astrakhan on Wednesday, the 14th. We were greeted with hurrahs at each of the villages we passed, and our olfactory nerves were much offended by the large quantities of putrid fish with which some of them had filled their boats. Astrakhan is a large town, built along an arm of the Volga, with a branch of the river running through it, over which some bridges are thrown. It has several mosques for the Tartars and a fine one for the Persians. We found there a large number of vessels of all kinds, and saw many windmills. Crowds of various nationalities, Tartars, Russians, Persians, Cossacks, Circassians, Kalmucks, and others, thronged the ways and raised their hurrahs unceasingly as we proceeded up the river towards the landing-place, where a great triumphal arch was reared, and where new acclamations met us. The notables of the place were there to welcome us, as is their custom with sovereigns, by the offer of bread and salt, the date of our arrival being engraved on the golden saltcellar and on the gilt-silver salver that contained them. We were hardly installed in the palace prepared for us, when we were invited to witness a display of the fire brigade of the town, and in the evening there was an illumination. We went to the theatre, which was very hot. The actors appeared to be made of pasteboard, and it was only by degrees we became sure they were human beings.

Next day, before continuing our journey, we received the notables of the place, visited the Persian mosque, and one of the others used by the Sunnī sect; we went also to see the relics of Peter the Great and Catherine—two boats built by that Emperor with his own hands, and an enormous wine-glass out of which he used to drink wine with Prince Menschikoff, ancestor of the prince now in attendance on ourselves. Peter's tools were there also with which he built ships, and specimens of old weapons of various kinds. Our passage by steamer up the river to where we met the railway was through a country so beautiful and so thronged with towns, villages, people, and cattle of all kinds, that it was impossible to take one's eyes from their contemplation for one instant. Herds of pigs innumerable, black or piebald, which the natives of these lands eat, were also seen. Next day, before arriving at

Tzaritsin, a telegram was received from Tehran, mentioning a hurricane that had happened there. We were thankful not to have been exposed to its fury on the open sea.

At Tzaritsin we were conducted to the railway and placed in a train of the Emperor's private carriages, specially sent for our reception, and beautifully fitted up with reception saloons, dining saloons, and sleeping apartments. This is our first journey by railway, and very pleasant travelling it is to get over five leagues in an hour. In the morning it became evident that we had been passing all night through a fine country. All around us was green and full of flowers; mares, sheep, pigs, &c., were everywhere; and at each two or three leagues, a populous village. We passed a great bridge over an immense river that falls into the Don, and many smaller. The stations that we came to were all beautifully built, and at each were trains ready for passengers or goods, with refreshment-rooms and all other requisites. We passed a forest of pines; and at one time our speed was such that the crows were overtaken and left behind.

At Faustowo we were met by Prince Dolgorouki, the Governor of Moscow, and there we dressed for our entrance into that city. On arrival we were at once driven to the Kremlin, thence to dinner, and to the opera, the dances and dancers of which it is impossible to describe. Next day we visited the Crown Jewel Office and Armoury, replete with objects of interest; then to the Lazaroff College; thence to a reception; and again to the opera. On the morrow we visited sundry other establishments, and then left for St. Petersburg, where we arrived and were most cordially received by the Emperor and his sons and brothers on the 20th of May.

During our stay we received and paid visits, accompanied the Emperor to the opera, to a review of 20,000 troops, to the Palace of Tzarskoe-selo, to a ball of the nobles, &c. We held a reception for the Representatives of foreign Powers accredited to the Court of St. Petersburg—General Le Flo, Ambassador of France; Lord A. Loftus, of England; the Prince de Reuss, of Germany; and Kyāmil Pasha, of Turkey, &c. We visited the Museum of the Hermitage twice; but each room would require days to understand. We assisted at a grand dinner of state with 170 covers, at which the Emperor gave my health as a toast, and I returned the compliment by proposing that of green trees, and are very pleasant. To the right were the preparations for the fireworks; on the left, tents were erected. Passing on a little we came to the landing on the left hand and alighted from the vessel. Officials, women and men, and carriages in great numbers were there, the people having come in them from the city to see the fireworks. The arrangement of the ground, the trees, and the walks in this place also is like that at Peterhof. We proceeded until we arrived at a very beautiful house, where the wife of the Heir-Apparent, the Heir-Apparent, the princes of the blood, and others, were found. We sat down a while, and the Emperor came; compliments and conversation ensued. He stayed a short time, when we mounted a carriage with the Emperor, the Heir-Apparent's wife, the Heir-Apparent, the wife of the Prince of Oldenburg, and other children of the Emperor, all together, and drove out a little to while away the time until it should be dark and the time for the fireworks at hand. My travelling companions followed in other carriages. The air was bitterly cold. We went on without stopping for about a league. Detached houses in great numbers were passed; the walks were all extremely neat and clean. Then, returning, we alighted and staid a little while at the same house; again mounting, we went to a tent we had seen before, in which were assembled a host of Europeans and Persians. Crowds of spectators also were in ships and boats, and on the banks of the water. We sat down within the tent. The fireworks were very beautiful, and comprised a novelty, our name too being portrayed in Persian characters, with the device of the 'Lion and Sun,' all correctly. After the fireworks we mounted a carriage with the Emperor and returned to that same house again; remained a while, and then, my carriage being ready, we mounted, and again passing by some delightful spots and beautiful summer residences, in front of the mint and behind the fortress, and over a very long bridge, we reached home and dined. The Admiral who to-day accompanied us from (St.) Peter(sburg) is a man of short stature, and he lost one hand by a cannon shot in the battle of the Alma, near Sebastopol. His name is Skolkoff."

On the 27th of May we received a visit from Prince Gortchakow, and had a very long interview with him. We then had our photograph taken, and in the evening went by train to Tzarskoe-selo to a banquet given by the Emperor, and to the theatre in the grounds of the palace. On this occasion the Emperor made presents to every one of my suite, either of orders, rings, watches, or the like. I, too, presented a horse to His Majesty, and another to the wife of the Heir-Apparent.

On the 28th His Majesty came to pay me a farewell visit, and accompanied me to the terminus of the railway that goes by Wilna and Königsberg to Berlin, where we took leave and parted.

"Among other objects of interest seen in Russia, are the great number of carriages in Peter(burg), tramways in the streets, and many beautiful dogs, large and small."

We passed a very long iron bridge over the Niemen. In the morning, as I slept, we passed through "a hole in a mountain"—a tunnel 400 cubits in length, as they told me. Shortly after, we came to another "hole," 1,400 cubits long, which we passed through in six minutes, "the darkness being like that of night." We then reached the Russo-Prussian frontier at a place named "Aidgone." We were met by the officers sent by the King of Prussia to be in attendance on us, the chief of whom was a "distinguished Adjutant-General" of the name of "Boien." We were long detained at the station, "which is very plain," for the transfer of our baggage from the Russian to the Prussian carriages. A breakfast had been prepared for my suite, who partook of it. I was in a small room, and for some time was occupied writing my diary. Men and women thronged to the windows to see, and scuffles took place among them. "Freedom in this place is much greater than in Russia." At last, all being arranged, we went to our carriage. The train here was the contrary to that in Russia; there was no passing from carriage to carriage; so that, once seated, no one could know anything of those in other carriages, except during the minute of a halt. The speed was somewhat quicker than in Russia. Everything is here different from what we have hitherto seen—the country, the people, the vehicles, the food. The country is more populous and flourishing. Wherever I look, are villages, men, horses, oxen, mares, sheep, meadows, sown fields, streams, and flowers of every colour. At one station we received several telegrams from Tehran, all of good import, thank God! We soon arrived at Königsberg, on the river Pregel, to which ships came from the Baltic—a small town, but very pretty, of 95,000 inhabitants. One thing cultivated in Prussia is rape, here seen by us for the first time to-day, 30th May. It has a yellow flower of a very pleasing shade, and is sown for its oil, which is much used for greasing the wheels of railway carriages, &c. We were taken to an ancient palace, 500 years old. The people, never having seen a Persian, marvelled at sight of us. The carriages and horses here are not equal in number and beauty to those in Russia.

From Königsberg to Marienburg on the Vistula the same populousness and flourishing condition of the country were visible on all sides. Sailing vessels were on the Vistula, cattle and cultivation everywhere; the stations of the railway have neat gardens; lilacs were in flower, poplars and willows by the water, firs and pines in the forests. They brought me something to eat in the carriage at one station; but my suite breakfasted in a room. Then we reached Custrin, a strongly fortified place, where a salute was fired, and we received the authorities.

At Berlin, where the number of railways and of engines, carriages, and trains surprised us,— where our train was taken over one bridge, under another, and made to twist about like a horse whose bit was guided by the hand of man,—we were met by His Majesty the Emperor of Germany, his son the Heir-Apparent, his brother the Prince Charles, his nephew Frederick Charles,—the captor of Metz, and others of the Royal Family,—as the Prince of Hohenzollern, to prevent whom from becoming King of Spain, France went to war with Germany; also the celebrated statesmen Prince Bismark, Marshal Roon, Marshal Möltke, &c. Seated in an open carriage with His Majesty, we drove through a wide street lined with old trees and white cluster-roses in flower, and filled with crowds cheering, to a place like a gateway, with no trees, with a wide avenue, and high buildings on each side. Here we saw a column recently erected in commemoration of the victories over France, but not yet finished. We passed the statue of Frederick the Great, in front of the University on our left, and on our right the palace inhabited by the Emperor now and before he came to the throne, and so reached the palace assigned to our use, in a square with two fountains playing. The Emperor conducted me over the apartments to my private chamber, where he left me. I shortly went to return His Majesty's visit, and was met at the foot of the stairs by him. His Majesty is seventy-six years of age, his brother is seventy-three; but each is strong and vigorous. The city is lighted with gas; the lamps being more numerous than those of St. Petersburg.

Next day, Sunday, June the 1st, went to Potsdam, and drove about the lanes, admiring the beautiful houses and gardens, the lilacs and other flowers, the birds singing in the trees. But, being Sunday, all the world was out too, and the throngs somewhat impeded our enjoyment. I then paid a visit to the Queen Dowager, at Sans Souci,—an old woman of seventy and upwards. Saw there, also, the room where Frederick the Great died, which is kept in the same condition as then, the time-piece even not having been wound up since. When Napoleon took the place, he tore the cover of the table of Frederick, which remains thus torn. We then went to see a ruined water-mill of the time of Frederick, which he could not persuade the proprietor to sell to him to complete his plans.

From thence we went to visit the wife of Prince Charles, sister of the Queen of Prussia, wife of the Emperor, and mother of Frederick Charles. I wrote my name in a book she brought. Went to call on the wife of Frederick Charles, but she was not in. Returned home, and dined with the Emperor, the Princes, and Marshals, &c.,

in the same palace. Marshal Wrangel, a little old man of ninety, who fought in the wars against Napoleon, was there, and with him I had some conversation. Thence with the Emperor to the Opera.

Next day, Whit-Monday, after receiving the Foreign Representatives and Prussian Ministers, went to the Zoological Gardens. Being a holiday, the crowds and the carriages thronged. I was much struck with the black-maned African lion, and would have liked to remain some time to observe him attentively, but the crowds prevented. The African elephant is very different to that of India, its ears being much larger and wider. The giraffes, zebras, bisons, long-haired oxen of Tibet, llamas, argalis, &c., &c., were all most interesting. The place is extremely clean, and the animals well fed, each with its own special food. Leaving this, I drove and walked about in many beautiful streets, squares, and gardens; even in a cemetery, which I mistook for a garden, and which was full of nursemaids and children, who thronged about me. General Boien, who is in waiting on me, performed the same office to Napoleon III when in captivity, and to the Sultan of Turkey.

On the morrow I visited the Empress Augusta, who had newly arrived. She inhabits the same palace as the Emperor. He was unwell. She is seventy years old. Thence to visit the Crown-Princess, eldest daughter of the Queen of England, and saw also her three sons and two daughters, the eldest being fifteen years old. Thence to see the aquarium, where I met the Crown-Prince. The wonders of this place, fitted up as a rocky cavern in a mountain, with reservoirs containing marine plants, fishes, crustaceans, zoophytes, &c., is past description. An excellent collection of birds is also there seen. In the evening all our party dined with the Emperor and Court; whence to the theatre, and then home.

The day following, witnessed a review, dined with the Empress, and went to the large theatre, the whole audience being in Court costume. Also visited the Arsenal, with all its trophies, especially the great bronze lion of Denmark, brought from Holstein. One night, too, the fire brigade practised in front of our residence.

On Thursday, 5th June, the Insignia of the Black Eagle in diamonds were sent to me by the Emperor; went to Potsdam to a review, to the orangery, and in the evening to Babelbrig to dine with the Emperor and Court, and with the Crown-Prince to visit the tombs of Frederick the Great and his father, in Potsdam; thence to the Prince's house, where there was a reception and supper. The Crown-Princess wore the Order and Ribbon I had given her. On my way to the station, in returning, I visited a kind of Crystal Palace, illuminated.

On the 6th we went to the Parliament or State Council of Germany. About a hundred members were present. Prince Bismark was in his place at the right of the President's chair. The Under Minister for War was speaking on the question of the École-des-Cadets at Potsdam. One day the Crown-Prince, who was educated there, brought the Cadets, to the number of 700, and reviewed them in front of my quarters. On my way back, called at Prince Bismark's, who met me and presented his wife and family. A small, plain house. Thence to the Museum. Thence on a farewell visit to the Emperor, where I found the Empress also. To-day Prince Adelberg, a cousin of the Emperor's, and Admiral-in-chief of the German Navy, died on the banks of the Rhine, and the aged grandmother of the Emperor also died; for which reasons a concert, arranged for this evening, was put off. The Empress presented me with a china vase. Went to the aquarium, and attentively examined the sloth, which is also there. I observed that on his front feet he has two long claws, like those of an eagle, and on his hind feet three claws. Wherever he fastens himself, it is with difficulty that he moves. Thence went home.

On Saturday, 7th of June, left Berlin *en route* for Cologne and Wiesbaden. Passing by Hanover and through Westphalia, we reached the works of M. Krupp one hour to sunset. M. Krupp himself came to the station. He is an old man, tall, and very thin. He has, himself, gradually formed these works, and hence he furnishes cannon to every Government—guns for fortresses, guns for ships, guns for field use, all are made here. The works are like a city; 15,000 workmen are there employed, for all of whom he has built habitations, and to whom he pays wages. He has an income, clear of outgoings, of 800,000 tūmāns (400,000*l*. about). I went to see the steam-hammers, &c.; and M. Krupp made me a present of a beautiful 6-pounder gun, complete with all its appliances. We then proceeded to Cologne.

Next day, I visited the long iron bridge across the Rhine, and the Botanical Gardens. Here I saw tubes of india-rubber in use for watering the lawns and plants. Thence to the Zoological Gardens, where I saw many animals I had not seen at Berlin, especially some ostriches; also a white camel, male, in heat. It is singular for a camel to be in heat in summer. This day, Mr. Thomson, with one of my suite, proceeded to London. We went to Bonn, to Coblentz, where we crossed the Rhine, which is narrow here, the country being hilly. It is full of villages, with vineyards, cherry-orchards. The cherries were ripe, and very abundant. Every vine was bound to a stake, and the hills are one vineyard throughout, the wine of the Rhine being celebrated. The railways on both sides of the river, the common roads, the vehicles, the foot passengers, the flower gardens, the towns at short intervals, are all objects of wonder, which one does not tire with contemplating; it is like Paradise. On some of the hills are the ruins of old castles. In parts I was reminded of my first visit to Gīlān and the Safīd-Rūd. Sometimes we were carried over the tops of the roofs of villages and over streets. At length we left the banks of the river, and arrived at Wiesbaden, a city with hot mineral springs, and a place of great resort for strangers from all countries. The following day drove to Schierstein to see a manufactory of champagne, a kind of wine. Departing thence along the river bank of the Rhine, I saw a most beautiful garden within a dwarf wall and iron-railings. We stopped and rang; the gardener came, and we entered, with the German officials in attendance. The walks, the lawns, the trellises with vines, the roses and other flowers, and the view of the river, were charming. There was a bee-hive, basins of water with *jets-d'eau* fed from the top of a high tower of stone. The cherries were very fine. The door of the house was closed, but through the windows of the ground-floor I saw the rooms, furnished with chairs, tables, looking-glasses, &c., in perfect order. The place is the residence of a certain M. Blundberg, a private gentleman of wealth, who bought it for 33,000 ducats. He was away at St. Petersburg, and his wife at Wiesbaden, so we did not see them; but there were several elderly damsels, who brought us tea, bread, sweetmeats, &c. Thence I rode on horseback to Biebrich, a palace of the Duke of Nassau, who is at Vienna; but we met his brother, Prince Nicholas, with his wife, on horseback, who accompanied me in the grounds and a considerable distance afterwards. We passed through the town on our return towards

Wiesbaden. Next day I went by rail to Frankfort-on-the-Main, passing opposite to Mayence, the largest city on the Rhine. All the cities of Europe are alike; the description of one will serve for all; so I passed through the town to the beautiful suburbs, and visited the Palm garden, lately laid out. The palms are in a conservatory, but give no dates. From thence to the Zoological Gardens; not so good as at Cologne, but still very satisfactory. Saw a large elephant. They brought a grinding organ; the elephant turned its handle quickly with his trunk, and played a tune, to which he himself danced. The keeper then brought an instrument which children play upon with their mouths; the elephant took this also with his trunk, and began to sound it and to dance. It was a strange sight. Returned to Wiesbaden; drove to the suburbs, and up to the tomb of the wife of the Duke,—a Russian Princess; it is beautifully adorned, and has her recumbent effigy in marble on the tomb. All this country of Nassau and Frankfort, formerly independent, was lately conquered by Prussia, and Frankfort was made to pay a heavy ransom. In the evening, witnessed an exhibition of fireworks—very beautiful. At one of the gardens I saw a daughter of Malkam (Sir John Malcolm), the English

Ambassador to the deceased Kháqán (Fath-Ali Shah), of blessed memory; an aged fat woman, who has a daughter, very handsome; they now reside in Prussia.

Mirza Malkam Khan, who had remained behind in Berlin for the purchase of muskets, joined us again this evening; and to-morrow Dr. Tholozan goes to M. Krupp for the purchase of cannon. Opposite my residence is the market, and in the morning women bring fruit and vegetables to sell. Donkey-riding is much in vogue here, especially by the women, for hire.

On Wednesday, 11th June, went to Darmstadt, *viâ* Frankfort, on a visit to the Grand-Duke of Baden. By a singular coincidence, on arriving at the station, another train came in, bringing the Emperor of Russia from Vienna on his way to Ems. We had a cordial interview, and then we saw the Duke of Darmstadt, who is the brother of the Empress of Russia, and is independent of Prussia. A daughter of the Queen of England is the wife of his son or grandson, whose child lately fell from a window and was killed. We then went on to Heidelberg, where a Professor made a speech to me in Persian; then forward to Carlsruhe, and were met at the station by the Grand-Duke of

Baden with his Court. The troops are dressed in Prussian uniform, with a distinctive badge in their caps for Baden. They distinguished themselves greatly in the war with France. After dinner, accompanied the Grand-Duke to Baden-Baden, the country around which, and its climate, are very similar to those of Māzandarān. "It is the very Paradise of free-livers, sybarites, and lovers. Beautiful women, graceful ladies, for ever perambulate on foot, on horseback, or in carriages, the lovely walks and roads, the charming paths and lawns, of its hills and dales. It is a special corner, a city of fairyland." Prince Menschikoff, who was in attendance on us in Russia, has a house here, and was here himself, with his wife. They came and were received by us. We walked about the town, in the shops, and to see the fireworks. Crowds were everywhere; our purchases occupied a long time.

Thursday, the 12th, Prince Gortchakow arrived from Russia and was received in audience. Went to several of the baths, and had a dip in one. Walked in the streets, the weather being very gloomy, cold, and raining at intervals; had no overcoat, so climbed the hills to warm myself after the bath. Entered a church built by the ex-Prince of Roumania in memory of a young son who is buried here. His tomb is ornamented with his statue in marble. The ex-Prince and Princess now live here, and have built a tomb where they are to be buried, opposite that of their son. Their statues in marble are placed upon it; that of the Prince points with its finger to the tomb of the son. Returned to the Grand-Ducal Palace, seeing novel sights everywhere; thence again to Carlsruhe with the Duke, where we parted, and I returned to Wiesbaden. The Duke has three sons, his wife being a daughter of the King of Prussia; the eldest, the Heir-Apparent, is seventeen or eighteen years of age.

Friday, 13th June, drove down to the Rhine at Biebrich, and went on board a steamer to descend the river. Two of our people were belated, and did not reach the landing-place until we had left. They made all manner of signals, but those of the boat paid no attention, so we sent an official to bring them to Cologne by train. The river is very beautiful, full of life and traffic on the water and on shore. The hills on each side are not high, and are all cultivated. At Coblentz our boat passed under an iron bridge of three spans. Here the Sultan of Turkey met the King of Prussia and spent three days. It is a very strong fortress. A salute was fired. At Bonn we left the steamer, and, proceeding by train, passed Cologne towards Belgium. We went through fifteen tunnels, by Aix-la-Chapelle, to the Belgian frontier, where General Boien took leave. "A small stream separates Belgium from Germany, but what a sudden change in all things takes place there. The men, the language, the religion, the land, the water, the hills, the plains, all are different; nothing remains with the slightest resemblance to those of Germany. The hills are a little higher and more covered with forest; the air is colder; the language is French, though the people have a dialect of their own; the inhabitants are poorer; the dresses of the people and of the soldiery are different; the religion is Roman Catholic; they are more free than in Germany."

We arrived at Spa, and were suitably received and lodged. The town was illuminated in the evening, and we went out for a walk. The street is named "Seven o'clock." Went into some shops and made a few purchases, and then slowly home.

"The women in Germany are very laborious, especially in husbandry and horticulture, working harder than the men. The ears of the carriage-horses and others in Germany are covered over with red cloth, and the like, to protect them from flies. In Berlin and elsewhere the little boys in the streets take a soldier's musket on their shoulders, run about, play the fife, and thus beautifully become accustomed from infancy to a military life. The paving-stones are very well worked and joined. The bricks are like those of Tehran."

In the morning the Governor accompanied us in a carriage to the baths where Peter the Great had been treated. Outside the town we came to an establishment where the mineral water flows out of the soil into a basin. A woman stood there with a number of tumblers to serve the water to visitors. People come there before breakfast, drink the water, sit down, and then order food from the cook of the establishment. Many of the visitors are English. I drank a little of the water, which was very nasty. Outside of the basin there was a large footmark on the surface of a stone; the Governor said it was the print of the foot of St. Mark, "a holy man of the Franks." Every childless woman who comes and places her foot within this footmark becomes pregnant. "This is very singular; similar beliefs are very much in vogue in Persia." We then went to another spring in a different place; it was worse tasted than the first. I rode about on horseback, and met an English gentleman, with his wife, who had been long resident at Allahabad, in India. I conversed with them, and after taking leave, returned home by another road. A headache and shivering seized me—the effect of my taking cold after my bath at Baden-Baden yesterday. Dr. Dickson treated me, and Dr. Tholozan returned from M. Krupp's works. After a night's rest I was quite well again, thank God.

June 15th.—Being a holiday (Sunday) of the Franks, a number of maidens and matrons came from the street opposite my hotel and went into the church. Other girls dressed in white, and others again smaller, and boys in nice clothes, with tapers and nosegays in their hands, formed a procession; canopies were borne, with figures of the Virgin Mary and Jesus (on whom be peace), and the children and priests chanted a service melodiously. In the evening I walked to a small theatre very near to my hotel, where a crowd of men and women were assembled. The actors spoke in French; the subject was love and lovers. Then a juggler performed his tricks [*several of which are minutely described*] and his wife performed feats of clairvoyance after being mesmerized by him. I received here, at Spa, a Russian gentleman, M. Khanikoff, whom I had seen twelve years previously in camp at Sultāniyya, and who now resides at Paris; he was younger and better looking than ever.

June 16th.—Being now quite well again I left Spa for Brussels in the King's carriages, which had been sent for me. At the station I saw the wife of the juggler of last evening in the crowd assembled to see us leave. The Belgian trains shake and jolt less than those of Germany, and travel faster. Passed three or four tunnels, through forests, and by hill and dale to Liège, a place famous for its manufactories of fire-arms and railway stock. All the parts about here have quantities of a very pretty flower, resembling that of the bean, but yellow (perhaps the laburnum is meant). In three or four hours we reached Brussels, and were received at the station by His Majesty the King, his brother the Count of Flanders, and a numerous suite; left in an open carriage with His Majesty, saluted by the assembled crowds, and was conducted to my apartments in the palace by the King. I sent the decoration of my portrait to His Majesty and then went to pay my visit, when I was received by the Queen. Leopold II is a man of about thirty-eight years of age, tall, somewhat thin, with a long yellow beard. As a Prince he travelled in India, in Egypt, Syria, and to Constantinople. He is grandson to Louis Philippe, the former King of France, through his mother, that Sovereign's daughter. He is also cousin to the Queen of England. He has three daughters, but no son; his brother, the Count of Flanders, is his heir presumptive. The Queen was a German Princess, the Countess a Prussian Princess. Belgium is a country of great freedom; its affairs are ruled by the Parliament. This Assembly was then sitting. Forty-two years ago Belgium became independent, having been united to Holland before that time. Larenson Sâhib (Sir H. Rawlinson), Kambal Sâhib (Sir A. Kemball), Thomson Sâhib, and several other Englishmen sent to be in attendance on me, were here presented to me. Larenson was twelve years ago Minister in Tehran, and is now rather aged. In the evening went with the King to the opera, which is as large as that of Peter(burg). In the morning received the Foreign Ministers and those of the Belgian Cabinet. Then drove with His Majesty to see the city, the cathedral, the museum, the Château of Laken, the Canal by which ships come and go between Brussels and Antwerp, &c. Was received by the Queen at Laken, and I presented Her Majesty with the Order of the Sun, and the Broad Ribbon thereof. She put it on with her own hands. Went to the Hôtel-de-Ville to see the paintings and tapestries. Dined there in the evening with the King, grandees, and foreign Ministers, &c.

"*June* 18*th*.—Rose early, though I had had no sleep. Was accompanied by the King to the railway station with all military honours, and thence set out for Ostend, which was reached in three hours, passing through Flanders, where Flemish is spoken. Ostend is a commercial port of some importance, and many ships were there. The Belgian officials in attendance took leave, and those of Ostend had an audience, at which a very long address was delivered. Proceeded to the landing-place, and embarked on board Her Britannic Majesty's ship 'Vigilant.' Larenson Sāhib and the other Englishmen in attendance conducted the presentations and did the honours. An English Admiral of distinction, named MacClintock, who has made several voyages to the islands of the North Pole and is well known, having come to meet me, was in the ship, with many other naval officers. We went to our special cabin and sat down. The ship is very fast and handsome. The Grand-Vazīr, our private attendants, and some others, were in our ship; the princes, &c., were in two other vessels like her. We waited a long time while the luggage was being brought, and our fellow travellers dispersed here and there. Being tired from a sleepless night, I myself went to a lower cabin and took some repose. Then coming up again, I found on my table some beautiful fruit of various kinds, very fine peaches, excellent white and black grapes with a delicious perfume, bananas, which are very nice, and a small melon, very sweet. These are all raised in hothouses, and they sell at very high prices. For instance, one bunch of grapes is sold for 2s.; the rest may be judged of by this. We proceeded on our voyage. I breakfasted. They had given an excellent breakfast to my suite.

"From Ostend to Dover—the first of English soil—is a distance of five hours, and the Straits of Dover are famous for stormy and boisterous seas. But, thank God, the sea was very calm, like the palm of one's hand, so that no one suffered. It was like a trip on a river.

"Behind us, in our wake, three ships convoyed us; while two large iron-clads, men of war, kept their stations as a guard of honour, the one on our right, the other on our left. Now and then they fired a gun. After we had advanced a certain distance, another ship came with two turrets, and two guns in each turret. These turrets turn round in every direction as desired. This vessel, too, is an iron-clad, and has a steam-power of 5,000 horses. Her sides are not so lofty. They said the shots of the guns of this ship knock the other ships to pieces. They fired two or three rounds with her guns, which made a great noise. Many merchant ships and others came and went on their voyages; and at length we neared the English coasts, the hills of the shore becoming visible. Many men-of-war came to meet us. They all fired a salute. The surface of the sea was covered with ships and boats and large steamers, in which the merchants and nobles of England had come to witness the spectacle. The hills of the coast are not so very high; the rocks thereof are white, like a lime-quarry.

"At length we reached the port of Dover. They have built a long stone pier here to protect the ships in the harbour from the waves and tempests. It extends far into the sea. Upon it were numbers of men and women, ladies and gentlemen, troops of infantry and horsemen. Here we stood. The sons of Her Majesty the Queen of England, with Lord Granville—the

Secretary for Foreign Affairs, and the magnates and notables of London had all come,—the second son of the Queen, the Duke of Edinburgh, and the third, Prince Arthur. We stood up in the ship; the Queen's sons, the Foreign Secretary, the Lord Chamberlain of the Queen, who is a personage of consideration, and also First Officer of the Household, came. We went into the ship; we sat down in the cabin and conversed, until the baggage was landed. The Queen's second son is a very handsome and well-made young man, with blue eyes, somewhat of a beard, not very tall, and perhaps about twenty-seven or twenty-eight years of age. The third son is less, his complexion is rather dark, and his frame slighter. The Lord Chamberlain's name is Lord Sydney, a hale old gentleman.

"At length we rose and went on to the pier, where there was a great concourse and crowd. We entered a train. I, the Queen's sons, the Grand-Vazír, the Foreign Secretary, and the Lord Chamberlain, occupied one carriage. The carriages were very beautiful; no such carriages had been seen. We went on slowly a few feet, and then alighted at a building where they had prepared food. I went into a small room, and there gave audience to the Hakīmu-'l-Mamālik, who had been here some time. I was informed that the magistrate of Dover had prepared a speech, which he must recite. I went to a hall, and stood at the top of a high flight of steps. The English princes and magnates, the princes and officers of my suite, were present. The magistrate recited the address at full length. It contained much in our praise and glorification. We made a reply, which Larenson explained in English. The people clapped hands. We then returned to breakfast; all my suite were there. They brought hot dishes, fruits, &c., of which we partook. Then we arose and returned to the carriage, and proceeded on our journey, with the same personages accompanying us. The road skirted hills and valleys; we passed many tunnels, a couple of which were a quarter of a league long, very dark and suffocating.

"The country of England resembles no other. It has more forests, the trees are large, the population continuous, cultivation more abounding; and the wealth of the English is famed all over the world, so that we need not here write about it.

"We passed by the neighbourhood of Chiselhurst, which was inhabited by the third Napoleon, and where he died and is buried.

"The train proceeded with such speed that it was impossible for one to see anything. Through its extreme velocity fire came from the wheels, one of which ignited, and it wanted but little of being totally consumed. They stopped the train; they alighted; they put out the fire. All was well, and again we went on until we reached the first outskirts of London.

"It is impossible to describe the prosperity, the populousness, the great extent of the city, the number of railways, on which, incessantly, trains are passing and repassing, and the smoke of factories, &c. We went over the surface of the roofs of the houses, and so arrived at the terminus.

"We stood up; the crowd of spectators was beyond limit. Troops of the line, household cavalry in armour, His Royal Highness the Heir-Apparent of England—known as the Prince of Wales—all the Ministry, nobles, and notables were present. We alighted; I, and the Heir-Apparent, the Grand-Vazir, and Lord Morley—Lord in Waiting—took seats in an open carriage, and drove off. Both sides of the road, the roofs and upper stories of the houses, were all filled with men, women, and children. They showed much joy, and cried 'Hurrah!' They waved handkerchiefs, and clapped hands. In short, it was a strange hubbub. I incessantly, with head and hands, saluted the people; the crowd of spectators had no end. They say the population of this city is more than four millions (eight crores). Its women are very handsome. Nobleness, grandeur, sedateness, and self-possession flow from the faces of its men and women. One can see they are a great nation. The Lord of the Universe has especially bestowed on them power, and wealth, and wisdom, and sense, and refinement. Hence it is that they have subjugated such a country as India, and hold mighty possessions in America, and other parts of the world. The soldiers are very strong of frame, and well-dressed. The armour-wearing household cavalry are very strong, handsome youths, well dressed, like the cavalry of Russia. Their horses are strong and handsome; but their number is small. They are four regiments, each of 400 men.

"Half our journey was performed in the rain, which wet the people through. I, too, got very wet; but at my request the carriage was closed in part. The Grand-Vazír and Lord Morley remained exposed, and were drenched in consequence. And so we arrived at Buckingham Palace—my quarters, where we alighted. It is the town residence of the Sovereign, and is of great size and extent. The Heir-Apparent, and the other princes who had accompanied me, took me to my apartments. All our suite are housed here also. Behind the palace is a beautiful garden, with green lawns, well kept. They have an agricultural machine, like a cart, drawn by a horse, that cuts down the grass in strips a yard broad, which falls into the cart. There is a beautiful lake, with pleasure boats on it for pastime. There are also several pretty tents erected. In every corner of the garden are large forest trees and beautiful flowers. Several peacocks are there, and a crane was walking about on the lawn. I was very much worn and fatigued, so that I retired early to rest. The Sovereign is at Windsor Castle, six leagues from town; but one gets there in half-an-hour by train. On the staircases and within the palace are some old English soldiers, in the costume of four hundred years ago—the time of Queen Elizabeth—very quaint.

"*Thursday, June* 19*th*.—In the morning, paid a visit to the Heir-Apparent,—not far off. He has a nice house, and seven or eight sweet children. His wife is a daughter of the King of Denmark, and sister to the wife of the Heir-Apparent of Russia, who, with her husband, has recently come here on a visit, and will remain a month. I remained a short time, and we conversed. All the walls of the room, &c., were covered with hunting scenes, tiger-skins, &c.

"From thence I went to visit Prince Alfred, Duke of Edinburgh. He, too, has a nice house. The heads of stags and other game, the head of an elephant shot at the Cape of Good Hope, with many birds of beautiful plumage, dried, are collected in glass cases and the like. Equipments for the chase there were also. Prince Arthur was not in, having gone to a review.

"I next went to see the Duke of Cambridge, cousin to the Queen, who has a fine house. He is the Commander-in-chief of all the English land forces, and Special Commander of the Royal Artillery and Ordnance; an elderly man, but strong and hale, rosy-cheeked and fair of complexion, very pleasant of aspect, and much esteemed. After a little conversation I took leave, and went to visit his sister, wife of the Duke of Teck, who is a prince and noble of Germany, and a very charming young man. He wears small mustachios, and is well made. His house and garden are very fine, given to him by the Queen.

"We then returned to the Palace to receive the foreign Representatives and the Cabinet Ministers. Dressed in state, and went to an upper saloon, where the Princes of my suite and the Grand-Vazīr, &c., were assembled. The Lord Chamberlain came in with the foreign Representatives, who remained standing. One by one I addressed them. The Ambassador of Russia, Baron Brunnow, an old man, has been thirty years the Representative in London. Musurus Pasha, Ambassador of Turkey, is a Greek, and a man in years. M. Beust, Ambassador of Austria, old, intellectual, and a magnate, who was formerly Prime Minister of Austria, and is a German. The French Ambassador, Count d'Harcourt, is a French nobleman. The Minister from Japan was among the others. The Maharaja Duleep Singh, son of Runjeet Singh, so well known, was there also. He has been in England twenty years, the Government making him a large yearly allowance. He is a young man of pleasing manners, and speaks English. He had adorned himself with jewels and pearls. He is an Indian Prince.

"Next to them came the whole of the English Ministry, who belong to the Whig party. Lord Granville, the Foreign Secretary; Lord Gladstone, Prime Minister; the Duke of Argyll, Secretary for India, &c. I had a long conversation with Lord Gladstone and the English Foreign Secretary. They left, and we remained alone. We went over the upper apartments of the palace, which is a grand place, and contains many portraits and paintings of merit. In the evening went with my suite to dine with the Heir-Apparent, and met the Heir-Apparent of Russia, the wives of both, and the English Ministers; and thence to an evening party at the Duke of Sutherland's, an English nobleman, who has a yearly income of a crore (of tūmāns, *i.e,*, 250,000*l.*). The Duchess is a noble lady of intelligence. The house is a fine one; the assembly was very numerous. We sat on a chair in a long saloon. The women, the English Princes, the Nawwāb Nāzim of Bengal, with his son, were there. The Nawwāb, an Indian Prince, has been two years in London on some business. He is a grandson of the famous Tīpū Sāhib (*sic; read* Sa'ib). When the dancing was finished we went home.

"*June* 20*th*.—Dressed in state for a visit to Her

Majesty Queen Victoria, Sovereign of England, at Windsor Castle. Went in a carriage with the Grand-Vazir and Lord Morley. Great crowds lined the road, and the private carriages were beyond computation. We passed through Hyde Park to the station, where we found a train of great magnificence, the sides of the carriage being each one sheet of plate-glass. We passed by inhabited and uninhabited places and green fields, until Windsor Castle arose to view in the distance, like a fortress with four towers. We mounted carriages, as did the members of my suite, and descended at the foot of the steps of the castle. Her Majesty met me at the foot of the staircase. I took Her Majesty's hand, gave my arm, and we went up stairs, through beautiful rooms and apartments hung with paintings, to a special chamber, where we sat down on chairs. The Queen presented her children, relatives, and officers; we did the same with our suite. The Lord Chamberlain, who is the Minister of the Royal Court, brought the badge of the Order of the Garter set in brilliants for us; and Her Majesty, rising, with her own hands invested us therewith, and with the ribbon; giving us also a long stocking-garter. This is the most highly esteemed of the English orders, the history of which is as follows:—

"Among historians there are two versions received respecting the institution of the Order of the Garter by Edward III, of England, in Windsor Castle, in the year 1349 A.D. One is that it was in commemoration of the victory at Cressy, which broke the power of Philip IV of France. The other being that at a ball the garter of the Countess of Salisbury, the King's mistress, fell off, and raised a smile among those present. The King, through his zeal and love for her, lifted up the garter and pronounced the words, 'Honi soit qui mal y pense,' which to this day are inscribed on the garter of the Order; and added, 'This garter will I cause to be so highly honoured, that to obtain it all shall become covetous.' Thence it has become the first Order of the Kingdom, and is given to none but the Sovereign—the Ruler of the Order, to Princes of the Royal Family of England, and to foreign Sovereigns; and never more than twenty-six Knights of the Order, native and foreign, are allowed.

"I received this Order with due reverence, and we again sat down. I, too, presented to Her

Majesty the badge and ribbon of the Order of the Sun, set with diamonds, and the Order of my own Portrait; which Her Majesty received with due reverence also, and put on. We then rose and proceeded to table, where three of Her Majesty's daughters and her youngest son, Prince Leopold, who does not yet quit his mother, also took seats. Prince Leopold had come to the station to-day to meet me. He is very young, and nice looking, and was dressed in Highland costume, which is thus: the knees are bare up to the thighs. One of the Queen's daughters, sixteen years of age, is also still living with her mother, and has no husband. Two other daughters are married. The (Persian) Princes were present, the Grand-Vazīr, Lord Granville, and others. An excellent breakfast was served, beautiful fruits being on the board. Afterwards, Her Majesty took me by the hand and led me to a place of repose, where she left me, and herself went away. I remained a short time there. I saw in a small space opposite the castle some of the armour-wearing household Cavalry, with a regiment (of Infantry) drawn up. They are very fine Cavalry, and very select Infantry. The English troops, though few in number, are well clothed, well disciplined, well armed, and are very strong young men. The bands play well. There is a broad alley in front of the castle, a league in length, with two rows of large and ancient forest trees on each side, which are strong and green, and very lofty. The ground in general is all grassland, with flowers and herbage. We descended, mounted a carriage, with the Grand-Vazïr and the Lord in waiting, and drove down the alley. Our suite followed in carriages. There were crowds of men and women; comely women, with children, and grown-up people of the town of Windsor lined the road, rode, or drove in the avenues. It was a grand sight; but after we had proceeded a space the spectators were few. Then we saw a herd of deer, like a flock of sheep, perhaps 1,000 in number, which were loose in the avenues and on the grass, and pasturing in separate bodies. They did not appear to be very timid of man; but nobody can annoy them. They are really antelopes; or, perhaps, between stags and antelopes—beautiful creatures. The avenues and trees and grasslands had no end. We drove two leagues, passing other avenues like paradise, bordered by numbers of high trees, all in flower, white and red, &c., of a species like the oleander (*qy.*, rhododendron), and so beautiful that nothing could be conceived surpassing them. We arrived at a large lake, around which were many women and maidens. We passed the lake and arrived at a very pretty little building, the property of Her Majesty, where we alighted and partook of some fruit. Our suite had also arrived, and went to the station. We mounted a boat for a row. All around the water were parties of men and women. We remained a while on the water, where there was a miniature model of a man-of-war, with twenty-four guns of the size of swivels. We went over her, and then returned by boat to the building, remounted our carriage, and returned to Windsor by a different road through trees and lawns and herds of deer; went to the station for town, where the crowds were as in the morning; salutations went on until we reached home.

"The edifice of Windsor Castle is very ancient, and outwardly makes no great show of decoration. It looks like an old stone building, its stones being of the size of bricks. It has one large tower, and several smaller and high. But the interior is highly adorned and very pretty, besides being fitted with objects of interest. Its rooms, halls, and corridors are beautiful; and it contains a museum of arms and armour. The age of the Sovereign is fifty years; but she does not seem more than forty. She is very cheerful and good-looking.

"Being invited for this evening to the house of the Lord Mayor, Governor of the old city of London, for an evening party and supper, we mounted our carriage in the night, and proceeded thither. From the palace to the Lord Mayor's house was the distance of a league. In the roads and streets there was such an assemblage of men and women as baffles computation. They cried out hurrah! and I, on my part, incessantly saluted them. All the streets are lighted with gas. But, added to this, from the roofs and windows of the houses electric lights made the streets as clear as day. Some had illuminated with gas in various designs on the houses and elsewhere by way of decorating the town and streets. We passed by large public buildings, by most enchanting shops, and by open spaces, to the ancient gate of the old city of London, of which the Lord Mayor is the governor, but has no authority over the other cities and boroughs. These have no governor; but each parish has its vestry, and if anything occurs that falls within the province of the chief police officer of the parish, who is the patrol officer thereof, he reports the same to the Home Secretary. The police of this city are 8,000 in number; all handsome young men in uniform. The public hold the police in great esteem. Any one insulting the police is liable to be put to death.

"Arrived at the door of the Lord Mayor's house, we went up some steps where there was a hall in which the Heirs-Apparent of England and Russia, with their wives, and all the foreign Representatives, and the Princes, &c., of our suite, the other Princes and Princesses, ladies of rank, magnates, and Cabinet Ministers of England were assembled. We exchanged compliments with the two Heirs-Apparent. This is a Government building, where the Governor of London resides. It is called the Guildhall. Once a year this Governor is changed at the election of the inhabitants of the city. The members of the Council wore a strange costume, with great caps of sable fur on their heads, with sable-lined robes, &c. In the hand of each was a long thing wand of wood, and in the other hand an old-fashioned small-sword. They formed a procession before us. We remained in that room, and the Lord Mayor made a speech, to which we replied. After which, with like ceremonies, we were ushered into a very large hall, with chandeliers and gaslights. We had given our arm to the wife of the Heir-Apparent of England. There were very many men and women, 3,000 having been invited for this night. The Lord Mayor wore a robe with a very long hind-skirt that trained on the ground. We went to the place of honour of the assembly, raised by a few steps, and sat on a chair; the wives of the two Heirs-Apparent being seated on either side of us: all the others remained standing. The Lord Mayor read an address in English, felicitating us on our arrival and on the friendly relations subsisting between the two States of England and Īrān; and gave a copy thereof, printed in Persian, to each of those present who knew Persian. After this recitation by the Lord Mayor, the Grand-Vazīr read aloud, with perfect elocution, that Persian version (to us), and we made a reply, which Larensen Sāhib interpreted. The formal part of the meeting being thus concluded, they gave into the hands of each person a gold pen, with ink, and a paper on which names were written, so that each one might inscribe therein the name of whomsoever he might wish to dance with.

They also presented as a gift a gold casket. Then the dancing began, and I continued seated and looking on. The two Heirs-Apparent, with their wives, &c., all danced. After the dance, again giving our arm to the wife of the Heir-Apparent of England, we went to supper—a kind of dinner after midnight, through halls and rooms and passages and staircases, all crowded with men and women, and all decorated with flowers, and shrubs, and trees, grown in pots, to a large apartment where the table was laid out. About 400 persons were at the table. An individual, of the inhabitants of the city, and deputy to the Lord Mayor, stood behind me, and every now and then in a loud voice gave notice to those of the company that they should prepare to drink, so that when the master of the house drank wine to the health of the great, they should rise and drink (also). The Lord Mayor first drank to our health. Then the Heir-Apparent of England gave a toast, and then again the Lord Mayor. Each time that individual gave notice beforehand to those of the company. After supper we all went home to bed; but on the way back, though it was midnight, there were the same crowds. This evening the Lord Chamberlain and the Grand-Vazīr accompanied me in the carriage.

"The Queen has a book in which every person who goes to Windsor Castle inscribes his name. I, too, wrote mine to-day.

"*June* 21st.—Went to visit Woolwich, the arsenal of England, a two hours' drive from the palace, through the town and inhabited quarters. Woolwich is itself a town, but is really a parish of London, the houses of which reach it. We started in the morning, the Princes and Officers of our presence being of the party. We crossed the river Thames by a bridge, and went through streets and roads of the outskirts, principally filled with butcher's shops. Workmen and labourers were passed whose faces were black with coal-smoke, and at length we reached Woolwich, a place of importance, with barracks for cavalry and infantry, and on the banks of the Thames. The Duke of Cambridge, Prince Alfred, Prince Arthur, General Wood—the Commandant and Military Governor of Woolwich, with other Chief Officers of the Royal Artillery, of Infantry, &c., came to receive us and lead the way. We drove on to see the factories, which are at a considerable distance from the public streets and roads. Crowds lined the way and cheered, while I saluted in return. We alighted at the workshops, and entered. It is now the system not to cast cannon in moulds; but, by means of machinery they possess, they make sheets of iron into tubes of the required size; these are taken to another shop and placed under steam hammers to be welded and beaten, and to be turned. Thus they become cannon. They told me this system was in greater estimation. We saw various workshops, one after another. In one they draw out rifled cannon, in another they cut, in another they bore, in another they hammer. They have arranged a large number of old and now useless guns in front of the workshops, and they have collected a multitude of shot and materials, this place being the arsenal for all England. After going about and approaching the furnaces, which were somewhat warm, we remounted and returned to the building we visited on first arriving. Here they had prepared a breakfast. It is a hall in which the land and sea and artillery officers breakfast,—a nice place. We took breakfast, and then mounted our horse and went with the Queen's sons, the Duke of Cambridge, and other officers, to a grassy plain to witness the artillery exercise. It is not very extensive, but at least 20,000 men and women had posted themselves around the plain and grassland to see the spectacle. Seventy pieces of artillery, of large size, were there. According to what they said, these guns had recently arrived from India, and would return there. The artillerymen and officers were well dressed. The English guns are after the old plan, muzzle-loaders; not like those of Krupp, breech-loaders. The foot and horse artillery passed before us; then a second time, at a trot; then at a canter, and then at a gallop. They then loaded and fired. They also made me a present of a 9-pounder gun. After this we returned home by the same way we had come.

"In the evening we dressed in State, and, accompanied by the Queen's Master of the Horse, who is a person of importance, and the Lord Chamberlain, we went to the theatre through the usual crowds and salutations. The Heirs-Apparent of England and Russia, with their wives, the other Princesses and Princes, and the grandees were all there. The theatre is very large, with six tiers of balconies, and very beautiful. They gave some good scenes, and the actors were numerous. Patti, one of the renowned singers of Europe, had been specially sent for and brought over from

Paris. She sang very well. She is a handsome woman. She took a heavy sum and had come to London. There was another, also, named Albani, from Canada, in America, who sang and played well. At length we rose and went home.

"*June* 22nd.—After breakfast went to the Zoological Gardens, two of my suite being with me in the carriage, the others also accompanying. Being Sunday, the streets were a solitude. All the people were in the fields, &c., for a walk. A few thousands were seen who were sleeping on the grass; but, when they saw my carriage, they came running from all quarters and cheered. The way was at a distance from the streets and shops. We alighted at the gate of the Gardens. There were many carriages in the park and road, and it was evident that many had come there on account of its being Sunday. The Director of the Gardens, an old man and hard of hearing, came to us. He knew a little French, so I conversed with him. The men and women were in great numbers; we passed through a narrow lane between them; they continually cheered. Really they have a love for us in their hearts! And, beyond all limits do they show their respect and politeness.

"The wild beasts here are in cages, apart. We saw several that we had not seen elsewhere. First of all, the hippopotamus—the river horse. He is a wonderful creature. There were three of them, a male, a female, and a young one born in the Gardens, and already of a large size. He was out of the water, the other two were in it. People threw eatables into his mouth. He opened his mouth like a gateway. His teeth were very rough, and his body was enormous. From what I saw, I conclude that the hippopotamus is the rhinoceros of the waters. Secondly, there was a very large monkey of most ugly appearance, exactly like a human being; his hands and feet in particular were very similar to those of man. His keeper made him dance. He stamped on the ground, it rose up; he said something in English, it understood; then it walked before us; but it continually showed an inclination that they should take hold of its hands and lead it. They then put him into the monkeys' cage, where his springs and climbing were prodigious; he was like a rope-dancer. Thirdly, there was a sea-lion and a sea-fox (seal); both in a tank of water with stone parapets. A man spoke to them in French, and they quickly comprehended. The sea-lion is very large, and his body is covered with a fine down; its fore and hind feet are like the fins of a fish and the wing of a bat; but it can run very fast. On the side and in the middle of the tank there was a platform on which they placed a chair; it got up and seated itself on the chair. The seal was like the sea-lion, but smaller. They went under the water; their keeper made a sound, and instantly they came out of the water on to the platform, and embraced their keeper, who had seated himself for the purpose. He said: 'One kiss,' or, 'Two kisses;' as many kisses as he asked for, they gave him. It was well worth witnessing. Fourthly, we saw some very small monkeys, not larger than a jerboa—very curious. There were also elephants, rhinoceroses, maned lions, tigers, &c., and birds and parrots of all colours. Besides these, there were many places to visit, but I got tired and could no longer walk about. The crowds, too, were great; so I returned home.

"*June* 23*rd*.—Having to go to-day to see a review of the ships of war at Portsmouth, I got up early, and, though tired from want of sleep, dressed and mounted the carriage and set out on the journey, accompanied by the Grand-Vazīr, the Princes, and others of my suite. Portsmouth is one of the principal English ports for ships of war. There were crowds at the station from which we were to start. I was detained in the carriage for some little time until the Heirs-Apparent of England and Russia, with their wives and others, came. They took their seats in another carriage, apart from me, and we started. The whole of the road was through cultivation, green and pleasant, or pine forests. In less than three hours we arrived at our journey's end. Portsmouth is a town of importance, and a vast military harbour, furnished with forts and bastions of great strength. We alighted at the landing-place. The Mayor and his Council came and made a speech; presentations were also made, and very many guns were fired on shore and on the water. We went on board the 'Victoria and Albert' royal yacht—very large, swift, and beautiful; also the two Heirs-Apparent, the Princes, some naval officers, and others. The name of the captain of this ship is Prince Linoge (*sic*). A breakfast was laid out in the cabin, to which we sat down. Then the Heir-Apparent of England said it was time to go on deck, as the ships were about to salute. We did so. There were also two young sons of the Heir-Apparent, dressed as sailors. Ships of war to the number of about fifty tillers, were anchored in two rows, like a street in the sea. They fired a salute. The men went on to the yards and shouted, crying hurrah! Other spectators from London and the coast, who had come to see the sight in great numbers, were in steamers and boats, large and small, so that the sea was black with them. They, too, shouted hurrah! They had hoisted the Persian flag on board each ship. It was a commotion.

"We went near to the Isle of Wight, a pretty Island in the English Channel. A town thereon, at the foot of a hill, and named Ryde, came in sight, the handsome houses of which were in tiers, one above the other. The Queen has a residence in this island, built by her and her husband, and named Osborne. We saw it at a distance. Outwardly it has a fine appearance, being on a hill and surrounded by a forest and grasslands. Passing by there, we went through the street of ships of war. They all fired a salute. Subsequently we went in a boat to visit two of the ships; first to the 'Agincourt,' the largest of all the English ships of war, and commanded by Captain Phipps Hornby, with a great number of officers. The ship was more than 150 feet long (sic), with a steam power of 15,000 horses (sic). Her guns were very large, some on an upper tier, others on a lower deck. We went below and saw all over her, even to the kitchen and the feeding place of the sailors and others. They blew a fife to make ready for battle. In an instant all the sailors came from above on to the lower deck, and with the greatest speed went through the gun exercise. They turned those enormous guns about with the implements of which they made use, so as to astonish us. There were about thirty guns of that large size. The ship is armoured. Thence we went by boat to another ship, the 'Sultan,' which is also very large, and is armoured on both sides. Her nākhudā (captain) is named Vansittart. She had fewer but very much larger guns. We then returned to our own ship. In the boat with us were the Heirs-Apparent of Russia and England, with their wives, one of my suite, the Duke of Cambridge, and others. A small steamer towed us. On reaching our ship it passed the ladder and went on under the very paddle-wheel, which was in motion. We had a narrow escape of being struck by one of the paddles; had this happened we must all have been drowned. Thank God, however, the wheel was stopped; we escaped the danger, got on deck, and returned to Portsmouth, where, in a room, another breakfast was laid out, of which we partook. We then mounted a carriage and went to see the workshops where they make all the fittings of the steamers and sailing ships, which was a great sight. Thence we went up a scaffold where they were constructing a very large ship of war, into which we went. The artificers were at work. They had called the ship 'Nāsiru-'d-Dīn Shāh.' Then we went to the railway and returned to town, arriving at about sundown.

"In the evening we went to a concert of vocal and instrumental music given in a building called the Albert Hall. We drove through Hyde Park, and at the Hall we met the two Heirs-Apparent, with numbers of English officials and others. First of all we went through a corridor six or seven cubits wide, and covered in with glass. It appeared to be of iron. Both sides were lined with machines, used in manufactories, small, like models, but very well made and beautiful. They were working by the power of a steam engine. We saw many manufactories, sweetmeat-making, cigar-making, tobacco-cutting, maccaroni-making, lemonade-making, soda-water making—where the bottles are filled and corked in a moment, turnery, Tunbridge-ware, silk-spinning, cloth-weaving, printing of a newspaper, and many others; all were performed with great facility. It was very complete. The presidency of this exhibition is in the hands of English noblemen, such as Lord Granville—the Foreign Secretary, &c.

"After mounting many stairs, accompanied by the two Heirs-Apparent and others, we arrived in halls hung with oil paintings, the most beautiful we had yet seen anywhere. The president over these paintings is Prince Alfred, son of the Queen of England, who is also Chief of the Navy. They are painted from their own imaginations by naval officers and officials who send them here. Leaving these, we passed by corridors, where are exhibited for sale the wares manufactured in the hall below. Women and pretty maidens, some employed in those manufactories, some on duty as saleswomen here, were seen and passed ere we arrived at a scene like paradise. The whole of these galleries and corridors and manufactories were lighted with gas in different beautiful devices. The concert itself was in a very large enclosure with a domed top, very high and very wide. It has seven tiers of galleries, all with seats for spectators, and all filled with women of graceful appearance and richly dressed. It was an assembly of the noble and the great. The pit also was full of men and women. The place was ablaze with gaslights. We went down. In the midst of this assemblage chairs were arranged; there we took our places with the two Heirs-Apparent, the grandees of Persia, the Ministers and notables of England, all in order. In front of us was a very large organ, as big as a palace, with iron columns and pipes, out of which came notes like those of musical instruments. It was a huge structure, of the size of a plane tree, built along one of the walls of the hall. Right and left of the organ were 800 beautiful women and maidens, 400 on each side, seated in tiers, and all dressed in white: 400 wore blue sashes over their shoulders, and 400 red sashes. Above these were 800 children, boys, nicely dressed, who sang to the notes of the organ and orchestra. The organ was played by one performer. Its sound went far. He played extremely well; but the wind of the organ is supplied by steam; otherwise how could one man blow it with his feet, or with his hands? There was also a numerous orchestra on the lower tiers of seats. Such an assembly was never seen before since the first of the world until now. There were 12,000 present, not one of whom uttered a sound; all quietly lent ear and looked on. It lasted above an hour, then we went home.

"*June 24th.*—We had to go to-day, at two in the afternoon, to Windsor Castle, to witness a review of troops to be held by the Queen. In the morning the Minister for India, the Foreign Secretary, and the English Prime Minister, had an audience with us that lasted an hour and a-half, at which the Grand-Vazīr was also present. It passed off pleasantly. We went to breakfast; but the Grand-Vazīr came and represented that the Minister for India was waiting to present his Councillors; also, that the inhabitants of the towns of England had come with an address felicitating us on our arrival, which they wished to deliver. We went to the saloon. Deputations were come from the large towns of England, and they presented an address. The members of the Persian Mission to England were then received. The Jews of London, the Magians (Parsees), the Armenians of Manchester, &c., had each an address and a speech, which they presented. Then the Minister for India presented his Councillors, who were numerous; among them particularly was Goldsmith—who had gone to the frontiers of Sīstān and Balūchistān, Smith, and the telegraph-men of Tehran, and others.

"We then proceeded in our carriage to the

station. The two Heirs-Apparent, with their wives, and the most part of our suite, were there, and accompanied us to Windsor. In effect, Windsor Castle is a fortress of strength, built in days of old, of stone, and placed on a hill. We alighted at the foot of the staircase, to which Her Majesty again came to receive me. We took each other by the hand, and all went upstairs, where we remained a short time. Then I descended with the two Heirs-Apparent, and we mounted on horseback. English generals and officers, with a squadron of cavalry, preceded us, and we rode down the long avenue in front of the Palace, at the end of which was an open space used as an exercise-ground. The ground was a league to go over, and both sides were so densely crowded with men and women that it was next to impossible to pass. They cheered so as to frighten the horses of our escort. These set up mad pranks; my horse, through its long travel and the fatigue to which it had been exposed at sea and on the railways, showed no signs of running away, but kept quiet. So we arrived at the end of the avenue near the exercise-ground. There we stood until the Queen should arrive with the wives of the two Heirs-Apparent, who were with

Her Majesty in one carriage. When they approached, we again pushed forward, and the Queen followed us to the exercise-ground. This was a vast lawn, surrounded with trees and forest. On one side, in form of a semicircle, men and women, spectators, were massed in countless numbers. Ten or fifteen pretty huts of wood, like tents, had been erected in a row, where the grandees and nobles, men and women, were seated tier upon tier. The flag of the Lion and Sun, with the English colours, was planted everywhere in front of this semicircle. Two large flags also, one Persian, the other English, were hoisted in the centre, where we were to stand. In fine, we arrived and stood under the flags. The Queen also came and stood. Presentations were made to Her Majesty in the carriage. Then I passed in front of the troops with the Heirs-Apparent, the Duke of Cambridge, &c.; we returned and took up places behind the Queen's carriage. The sky was cloudy and threatening to rain. We thanked God that no rain came. There were seven or eight regiments; three or four of the Guards, most beautifully dressed, with enormous caps of bearskin, &c., looking very terrible. These regiments were very fine. There were two regiments in Scotch costume, another named after the Heir-Apparent of England, and said to be archers (arrow shooters, perhaps riflemen), the Horse Artillery, Cuirassiers of the Guard, Hussars, all very fine, and together about 7,000 or 8,000 men. They went through their evolutions admirably, circuiting the ground several times. They then opened fire. With my own hand I gave a jewelled sword to the Duke of Cambridge, Commander-in-chief of the English forces. A good deal of conversation was held with Her Majesty; and when the review was over, near sun-down, we returned to Windsor Castle with the two Princes and the Duke of Cambridge, rested about half-an-hour, had an interview of adieu with the Queen, and returned to town, being invited to dine with Lord Granville at the Foreign Office, and assist at a ball. The Prince and Princess of Wales had also been invited; but, being over-fatigued with the review, telegraphed from Windsor to be excused from the dinner. We, therefore, dined at home, but went to the ball, where the Princes and their wives came also. Lady Granville met me, and I went upstairs holding her hand. The Foreign Office is a grand building; flowers and shrubs were disposed everywhere on the staircase and corridors. All the English nobility and foreign Representatives, with their wives, were there. I sat down a little, then went round the apartments with Lady Granville, took leave, returned home, and went to bed.

"*June 25th.*—To-day we are to go to Greenwich, which is not joined on to London, and is not separated from it, being on the banks of the Thames, and an outlying parish of the capital. We rose early; the Grand-Vazír was not in, so we mounted a carriage with one of our Princes and the Lord in Waiting, and drove to the city, the ancient town of London, down Regent Street, where there are some fine shops. All the shopping is done here; it is a noted place. The crowds and the carriages were so thick that one became bewildered with astonishment. We went through other streets also, and arrived at the ancient Tower of London. The Governor of the Tower, who is a General, with all the notables of the city, was there. The walls and turrets are all of stone, and the jewels, arms, &c., of the ancient Kings are kept there. We wished to see them, but there was no opportunity. We went on the river-bank, where there was a battalion of troops, with their band, &c.; also crowds to astound one. They had carpeted the river-side and hoisted their flags. Officials and grandees were there. A large and beautiful steamer had been prepared for us. The two Heirs-Apparent with their wives, and others, had arrived before us and were in the steamer. All our Princes, too, were with us. We went on board. The air was very cold, with a bitter wind. The smoke of steamers and manufactories came into the ship. The river is a tidal stream. There is an increase of water in the morning until noon, with a decrease in the afternoon of one or two cubits. Of the English, Dickson, Thomson, and Larinson, &c., were there. Our ship went first; that of the two Heirs-Apparent followed. There were so many spectators on the steamers and sailing-vessels, they could not be counted; also in large and small boats; all followed us. We went through the middle of London; both sides of the river are covered with buildings, manufactories, and high warehouses. We entered a dock. A dock is a number of basins that have been made for ships. They repair merchantmen and other vessels there; and, having anchored there, they take in their cargoes of merchandise or discharge them.

There are warehouses built round the dock, furnished with immense mechanical appliances, and therewith the cargoes are easily loaded or unloaded. For these docks there are gates of iron to the river, which are easily opened and shut when ships enter or depart. They are narrow, so that large ships enter with difficulty. We saw so many ships and so many spectators, that one wonders where they all come from. All are well dressed; the women are all handsome.

"Leaving the dock, we proceeded down the river through crowds in no wise diminished, some accompanying us in ships, others standing on the banks. Everywhere they fired cannon; and so we reached Greenwich. This is the Naval College of England,—a noble edifice, which we entered. The house of the Minister of Marine is also a very large old building. It is 200 years since it was built. The two Heirs-Apparent and their wives were there. In this hall were the portraits of ancient leaders, and paintings of naval combats. It has a dais, raised a few steps, where they had laid out a breakfast for us, to which we sat down with the Princes. The table for the others was very long; many sat down and breakfasted there. After breakfast they showed us the blood-stained garments of Lord Nelson. A ball struck his epaulette and passed down by his bladebone. His white vest, soiled with blood, was inspected. These are preserved in a case. The fight is called the battle of Trafalgar, where the English engaged the French and Spaniards; and, though Lord Nelson was killed, the English gained the victory. The Princes and their wives now took leave and returned, as we wished to visit the Observatory.

"We went first to the square of the Naval College, in the middle of which was a large man-of-war, with all its equipments, for the exercises of the naval boys. About 500 of these were drawn up in line, whose exercises we witnessed for a short time; after which, we drove to the Observatory, a kind of tower on a hill, with stone steps to go up. Large telescopes are there mounted in turrets, which can be turned round by machinery, so that the telescopes point in any required direction. It has a chief astronomer of reputation, who has often ascended in a balloon. The view over London and the river was very beautiful. We came down, drove to the landing, mounted the same steamer, and started on our return. Being now afternoon, the action of the tide made it low water. Not having to visit the docks, we went straight on our way, and passed under several bridges of iron and of stone until we reached the Houses of Parliament, which are in one wonderful building of great height, with still higher towers. They say that 12 crores (6,000,000*l.*) were expended in the erection of this building. It is on the right bank of the river (in ascending), and opposite, on the left bank, is St. Thomas's Hospital, also a very grand edifice. Crowds were standing to see us as we drove home.

"At night there was a ball in the upper apartments of this palace, our abode. We went up there and everybody was there. We took the hand of the wife of the Heir-Apparent, and went and sat down. They all danced. Afterwards a Scotchman came in the Scotch costume and played a bagpipe, which made a noise like that of a Persian horn. Prince Alfred, Prince Arthur, and others, danced a Scotch dance. Then the company broke up, and we went to another room to supper. They had laid out food, fruits, &c., on the table, of which all partook. The Indian Prince was also there. Then we went down and retired to rest, having to go next day to Liverpool, Manchester, and Trentham Hall, the seat of the Duke of Sutherland.

"*Thursday, June 26th.*—Rose early and drove to the station with one of our Princes and Lord Morley; the Grand-Vazīr, the other Princes, and the greater part of our suite remaining behind in London. Passed through Regent Street with its fine shops full of everything in the world. We saw also in that street a very large hotel, chiefly frequented by Americans. It is called the America Hotel (*sic*). We reached Liverpool in five hours from London, being a distance of fifty leagues. Our road passed through many tunnels, the country being very hilly. Everywhere we saw woods, and pastures, and sown fields, and populousness. We passed many cities and towns, that of Stoke, famous for its potteries, being among them. It is there they make the china-ware of England. Near Liverpool we passed through a very long tunnel, occupying five minutes in the transit. Almost in contiguity with it is the Liverpool terminus, where immense crowds were collected. On our journey we passed over an enormously high bridge across the Mersey, which flows by Liverpool to the sea. This river is not very long, but it is wide and large.

"The Governor and other officials and magnates of Liverpool were at the station. The Governor drove on in front, and we followed; my two companions being seated opposite to me. Liverpool is a large commercial town and seaport; the chief part of its business being with America, for wheat and cotton. England does not produce enough wheat for the food of its inhabitants. A large number of emigrants,—English, German, and others,—embark here for America. According to what is ascertained, more than 200,000 emigrants per annum go from this port to America, of which not one ever comes back. Europe has a powerful company organized for sending emigrants away. Two large ships, full of emigrants, were anchored in the river, in front of Liverpool. They were to have sailed this morning, but waited to see us; they will start this night. One of them, named the 'Oceanic,' was very large, and had 1,000 emigrants on board.

"Immense crowds lined our way; and, as the streets were narrow, we could not pass easily. The 'hurrahs!' were deafening. There was not one old woman or child in the town that had not come to see the sight. Being a commercial and manufacturing town, there are many workpeople here. Compared with London, the number of poor here seen was very great, in whose countenances was marked the difficulties under which they exist. We alighted at a place called 'St. George's Hall,' a large building, in which a throne was placed on a dais as our seat. Many men and women were in the Hall. The Governor read an address, enlarging on the friendship of Iran and England, to which we replied, and Larinson interpreted. Thomson and Dickson were there also. We then drove to the Governor's residence,—very nice. We were kept idle a short while in a room, and a slight rain fell. Then we went to a large hall, where tables were laid out for breakfast; we partook of some fruit, &c. The Governor gave a toast, proposing our health. When breakfast was over, a large number of people assembled in the court and inclosure of the house. We went in front of a window and saluted them. Soon after we drove to the bank of the river, and mounted a ship, which took us all to the entrance of the sea and back. The river is very wide, and has a town on each bank. The air was cold. We then drove back to the station, through great crowds; and the same railway took us in three hours to Trentham, the seat of the Duke of Sutherland. The train stopped at the gate of the park, where the Duke, with his suite, received us. We went in a carriage through lawns, avenues, and flowers; we saw the same kind of deer as at Windsor feeding on the grass. The Duke has erected here and there houses for the gardeners, keepers, &c.; also a hotel and a small chapel. We reached the Castle and alighted. Went through some rooms to a conservatory in the middle of the house, expressly constructed, where we saw flowers and shrubs of many kinds, with palm-trees, &c., such as are seen in few places. In the middle was a small circular basin, with a seated female figure in marble above a fountain. The flowing water was very clear. The perfume of the flowers filled the place; especially, a species of large Japan lily, white and variegated, was very beautiful and fragrant. We smoked a huqqa there, and then went out into the grounds in front of the house, which are extensive, but the trees are small. Cypresses, pines, and trees like orange-trees, planted in vases and placed out in beds of flowers, were clipped into round-headed plants. The gardens, with flowers, deciduous shrubs and evergreens planted out permanently, and the like, are very extensive and beautiful. The walks, the lawns like velvet, and the fountains playing likewise. A long, tortuous, winding, natural lake is in front of these gardens, with several small islands laid out with walks, beds of flowers, and shrubberies, to which access is obtained by boats. Around the lake is an eminence, clothed with pleasant foliage of shrubs; and around all are walks shaded overhead with trees, with flowers and vines trained on trellises of iron: beyond which, again, are the Duke's hot-houses and conservatories, in which are many flowers and beautiful leaved plants from America and elsewhere; especially the banana, a pleasant eatable fruit, like a small fresh pumpkin, with a yellow rind,—when ripe, it tastes like a melon and is soft, and similarly may be eaten with the fingers. It is rather nauseous, and is named 'mūz'* in Persian or in Indian. It grows plentifully in Balūchistān and Makrān.

---

* The botanical names of "*musa paradisiaca,*" the plantain, and "*musa sapientum,*" the banana, are taken from this Eastern name, a corruption from Arabic "mawz," vulgarly "mōz." The Indian name is "kīla," generally written "kela." There does not appear to be a true Persian name for the plant or its fruit, though it grows everywhere along the south coast of that country; "kanār" is doubtfully given in some lexicons.

"There were also nectarines, white and black grapes, plums, strawberries, cucumbers, &c. All of these were seen in the houses in all stages of growth and ripeness, by means of the stoves and arrangements made, which the gardeners work. They open and shut the windows and the skylights with screws, at will, more or less.

"We returned to the house, and went over the rooms, which are grand, full of luxuries, and cheerful, with paintings. The Consul-General of England in Egypt had recently arrived; his name is 'Ostantene' (*sic*, for Colonel, now Major-General, E. Stanton, C.B.) 'Lord Chose by' (the Earl of Shrewsbury) was there,—a nobleman who has a house in the neighbourhood, with a garden, in the Swiss style; and also a gentleman named 'Cok' (*sic*, for H. B. Loch, Esq., C.B.), who, in the war of the English and French against the Chinese, had been made prisoner. He has a long, thick beard. I asked him about his captivity. He said the Chinese had tortured him exceedingly. There were also some English gentlemen, who have been for years the companions and fellow-travellers of the Duke. His brother, his nephew, and his son, also, were there. His son is named the Marquis of Stafford. His eldest brother's name is Lord Albert Gower;

that of the younger is Lord Ronald. In the evening, an excellent dinner was served; and a beautiful illumination was arranged. We walked about. There was a place fitted up to play at bowls. In the middle was a long and low plank, hollow inside; two sets of wooden bowls, large and small, and in great number, were placed there. The two sides of this line were planked over on the ground, ridgeways; on each side of this is a channel. The bowls must be thrown with force, so that they may go and strike certain marks collected at the other end. Every bowl that hits is taken away; and every one that does not hit falls into one of the channels. The players form two sets; one set plays on one side of the wooden line, the other on the other side, and several are posted at the end. When the bowls are thrown into this line, they come along of themselves to the players. The marks that are knocked over are set up again. We went to this place, and just then the Duke and others came there. I said to the Duke, 'Will you have a game?' In a moment the Duke and the others stripped, took off their hats, and played. It was worth seeing. The intendent of the Duke's house, named Raïte (*sic*, for H. Wright,

Esq., private secretary), had a short time before been accidentally shot in the leg, and limped.

"*June* 27*th.*—After breakfast, went by train to Manchester, leaving most of my suite at Trentham. The train went very swiftly and passed through several dark tunnels. I went first to the works at Crewe, passing from the main line by means of a very small steam carriage, travelling on a special branch that went into the manufactory, and was a very pretty new sight. At these works they make engines and locomotives and railway carriages. With great facility do they wield large masses of hot iron; saw them, while red hot, put them under rollers and make them into plates, into long bars, thick or thin, for the manufacture of chains, like red snakes running along on the ground. For the welding of the plates of iron, hammering them, and joining them together, they have machines like two rams that butt at each other. They put the iron between these, and they butt it.

"We then went to another department where finer articles are made; and from thence returned to the main line and proceeded to Manchester, arriving there in two hours and a half from Trentham. There were more spectators assembled here than there had been at Liverpool. By reason of the multitude of factories here established, the walls and windows of Manchester are black as soot; the colour and complexion of the inhabitants and their clothes are black also. The ladies usually dress in black, as white or coloured dresses so soon become soiled. The magistrates and grandees of the city and environs were at the station, and we accompanied them to the Government House, where was a large hall. They had placed a chair at the top of some steps, and when I was seated, the Governor made a speech, to which I replied at some length, setting forth the friendship of Persia and England, and the pleasure and gratification I had experienced, from the moment of my landing in the island, at the honours paid and kindness shown by the Sovereign and the nation. Larinson Sāhib interpreted my words in English, which all approved. Then we went to another apartment where breakfast was laid out. This I tasted, and we then started to see a cotton mill. We passed along a very extensive street, crowded with people cheering so as almost to deafen one. This was from pleasure at seeing us. The mill we went to is of five stories, in each of which work was done, the greater part by women, spinning cotton yarn, &c. In the lower story, cotton cloth was being woven, which, in another place, is printed and becomes chintz, and is exported to all parts of the world. This lower story was something wonderful to see. It was as large as an extensive courtyard or square, and at least 2,000 looms were at work, each attended by four women. I passed by the whole of them. Suddenly the whole building was, as it were, shaken to its foundations by the united voices of women, girls, and men, who recited something in a very pleasing manner. When they had finished, we mounted our carriages and drove off to the station, and returned to Trentham at an hour and a half to sunset. The Duke received us, and we went on foot to see the deer in the park; then we got into a boat, and the Duke took upon himself the fatigue of rowing. We went about among the islands enjoying ourselves. After dinner there was another game at bowls, at which the Duke's son was the best hand.

"*Saturday, June* 28*th*.—Having to return to London to-day, and go to Chiswick in the afternoon, for a promenade party, as a guest of the Heir-Apparent of England, we took leave of the Duke and pursued our journey for more than three hours, passing by some towns and through numerous tunnels. Two of them were very long, each occupying five minutes to clear. We also passed through two long and narrow valleys (cuttings), the height of the hills not being great, but like two walls in steepness. The one wall all of rock, the other of rock and earth mixed. Hence become evident the great labour and expense with which these iron roads have been constructed. Reached the terminus at London, went home through great crowds, and one hour later started for Chiswick. This house and garden is the property of the Duke of Devonshire, one of the wealthy men of the English, and a relation of the Duke of Sutherland. He has lent it as a trust to the Heir-Apparent of England, that it may be his summer residence. The houses along the road were filled with spectators, as were the streets. The Grand-Vazir and Lord Morley were in my carriage. The drive occupied about an hour. Numerous vehicles were on the road, filled with those invited to Chiswick. We reached the gate of the garden by a private road, alighted, and entered the garden on foot. The Princes of our suite and others were there. There were several tents pitched on the lawn in the garden. The house is a poor (*sic;* apparently a misprint for 'small') building. We went into a tent where the two Heirs-Apparent and their wives, with many other ladies, the foreign Ministers, the members of the Cabinet, and others, were present. After a short time Her Majesty arrived; we went to her presence, and after a few words of conversation I accompanied the Heir-Apparent in a walk round the garden, charmingly laid out with flower-beds, and furnished with conservatories and hot-houses. All the company walked about. In one large tent eatables were set out in profusion. Everyone partook of something on foot. After this they prepared a pine tree and a spade in the garden, for me to plant the tree as a souvenir of my visit; and I did so. This ceremony is an observance in Europe, and a mark of respect to a visitor of distinction. We then went to bid adieu to Her Majesty in her tent, and she left for Windsor. We loitered a little longer, and then returned home by the road we had come. In the evening, being at leisure, we took our repose.

"The brother of the wives of the two Heirs-Apparent, Russian and English, who is a son of the King of Denmark, had newly arrived to-day. He is a youngster of about fourteen years of age, and is a naval officer. His name is Valdemir. We spoke together. He is come to see his sisters, and will leave in two days.

"*Sunday, June 29th.*—Cloudy, foggy, with violent rain. Took a drive in Hyde Park with one of our princes and Lord Morley. Although it was Sunday and no one was in the streets on account of the steady rain, still we saw many men and women there. We then took our road of yesterday to and past Chiswick, and drove on to Richmond, passing the botanical garden, where very many people were collected, but which we did not enter. It has a slender tower of great height, built in the Chinese fashion, of many stories. It is pretty, but we saw it from a distance. Arrived at Richmond, which is on a hill. It is not really a place apart, but is one of the suburbs of London. It has very pleasant walks, and a beautiful prospect over the surrounding country, especially of the river Thames. There were numbers of deer, as at Windsor. As the rain prevented our going about, it was proposed to take me to the house of Lord Russell, a former Cabinet Minister of celebrity, which was near at hand. I felt great inclination to go and see him. We went therefore. I alighted and entered. He and his wife came to meet me. He is an old man, nearly eighty years of age, short of stature, but, in spite of his years, clear and vigorous of intellect. He belongs to the Whig party. I must here explain; all the Ministers of England belong to one of two parties; the present administration being Whigs, of whom the chiefs are Lord Gladstone—the actual Premier, and Lord Granville—the Foreign Secretary, together with the other members of the Cabinet. The other party opposed in politics to these are called Tories, and their chiefs are Disraeli, Lord Derby, and others. Whenever the former quit office the whole Cabinet, &c., is changed, and those of the latter party take their places.

"We found M. de Beust, the Austrian Ambassador, and other political personages there. After a short interview, we proceeded to the hotel of Richmond, which is very handsome. A few years ago it was burnt, and has been rebuilt. The view was very extensive, but mist and clouds prevented its being seen to advantage. The rain, too, fell incessantly. We partook of tea and refreshments, and afterwards drove home.

"*Monday, June 30th.*—After breakfast the Tory Ministers came to an audience; also the Nāzim of Bengal, with his son; also Lord Russell, whom we visited yesterday at his house. (Sir G.) Seymour, too, was received, who, in the time of the late

Emperor Nicholas of Russia, before the war of Sebastopol caused a suspension of relations, was the (English) Minister Plenipotentiary at Peter(burg). Lord Derby and Lord Malmesbury, two former Foreign Secretaries of celebrity of the Tory party, were also presented. Then some merchants of India, &c., came, who were of strange appearance and oddly dressed. Chiefs of the Armenians, Jews, Christians, and then some people of the Punjab, in India, and others, came also. Among these was Iskandar Ahmad, son of the defunct Sultan Ahmad Khan, the Afghan, who had been for some time at Tehran with his father. He is a dashing young fellow, and an excellent horseman. He said he had been some years in Russia, but latterly he has resided in England. He had exchanged his Afghan turban and dress for the English costume, and came without a hat (on his head). He looked sallow and pale. Then came Lord (Stratford de) Redcliffe, of celebrity. He sat down, and a long conversation ensued. He is one of the great diplomatists of Europe, and for more than twenty years was the English Plenipotentiary at Constantinople, where he exercised great influence. In the Sebastopol war he forwarded the views of England and opposed those of Russia. He was in the service, though not in Persia, in the days of the first Napoleon, when Qardan Khān (General Gardanne)—the French Minister, left Persia, and the late Khāqān, Fath-Ali Shāh, of pious memory, received the English; according to what one remembers respecting those times, he must now be nearly eighty-five years of age. His mind is as vigorous as ever, but he is a martyr to gout. Were it not for this, he has, in my opinion, wit, wisdom, and strength of constitution enough to discharge any high functions to which his Sovereign might appoint him. We then performed our service of Divine worship. This evening we have to go to the Crystal Palace, outside of London, where there are to be fireworks and hospitality.

"In the morning, before the audience of the Ministers, the firemen came and went through their exercises in the garden in front of the palace. They planted ladders, with the supposition that the palace was on fire in an upper story. They climbed these ladders with all speed and agility, and saved several persons supposed to be, some burnt, some half-burnt, and some uninjured. These they either took on their backs and brought them down by the ladders, or slung them down with ropes. They have in this originated an excellent invention for saving human life. The strange thing is that while, on the one hand, they make these arrangements and take these pains to save life, on the other hand, in the factories, foundries, and works of Woolwich, in England, and of Krupp, in Germany, they invent new forms of cannon, muskets, and projectiles for the greater and swifter destruction of mankind; and he whose invention will slay more men in a shorter time plumes and prides himself thereon, and is decorated with orders.

"About the same time a set of English champions came and performed a boxing-match, which is an exchange of fisticuffs that demands great skill and agility; but they wear gloves of a large size stuffed with wool and cotton. Were it not for these gloves they would kill each other. It was very laughable and exciting.

"In the afternoon we drove to the Crystal Palace, the building in which the first Exhibition was held eighteen or nineteen years ago, and which is still standing. It took us an hour to reach it, but it rained heavily, and took away all pleasure. Still, crowds of men and women thronged our road and cheered us. We alighted at the door of the building, with the Grand-Vazīr, our princes, and suite. Outside of the building a tent was erected, where Prince Alfred, the Princesses, and a body of notables awaited us. They had set out fruit, ices, &c., for us there, and we were detained a few minutes until the two Heirs-Apparent of England and Russia arrived with their wives and others. We took the hand of the wife of the English Heir-Apparent and entered the building, when a surprising assembly smote our vision. On both sides of our path seats were arranged all over the place, on which beautiful women were sitting, richly clad, and men also, in tiers, leaving only a passage for us, so that we had to pass through them. The building is of iron and glass, so vast and so lofty that this evening 40,000 individuals were admitted by ticket. We went to the centre of the building, which is covered in with an immense and lofty arcade, in the middle of which is a basin of water arranged so as to appear a natural lake among rocks and hills, with a fine fountain abundantly flowing with water. To our left was an upper stage, and above that a balcony with many seats. I took a seat there, with the two Heirs-Apparent, their wives, the Princesses, and the Princes; the Duke of Cambridge being absent through an attack of gout. Facing us there was a large organ, like that of the Albert Hall, a numerous orchestra and singers. They played, they sang; and such a congregation was there, seated in that place on chairs, above, below, at the sides, and all around, that one became bewildered. They brought me a double opera-glass, and I looked about through it. Beyond the windows behind us there were fountains that played magnificently. The wife of the Duke of Sutherland, with her daughter, was sitting behind us. The Duke's daughter is very pretty. In front of us some Englishmen performed their gymnastic feats, very wonderful, leaping, climbing, and hanging suspended on a rope, &c., such as few could do. Then they brought Persian gymnastic clubs and played with them. After this a troop of Japanese came, men, women, and little children, dressed after the fashion of their own country, and performed some surprising feats, enough to make one go crazy in witnessing them. They work for the most part with their feet. They lay down, and they caused a large wooden box to revolve as they pleased like a bit of straw; they threw it up into the air, and again it fell on the soles of their feet. One of them, with his eyes blindfolded, lay down, and held straight upright, on the soles of his feet, a very long ladder. A child ten years old went to the top of the ladder and performed various feats; he threw into the air some curious balls, holding a case in one hand that had holes in it; and whenever a ball fell into a hole in the case, he, lying down in the same fashion, caused to revolve on the soles of his feet one of the folds of the lid (?) in a manner impossible to describe. A long thick rope was suspended from the vault of the arcade, which is 140 feet from the floor, and two or three English gymnasts performed thereon just as they liked. Seizing the rope they quickly ascended to near the vault and there stood slantwise on one foot; and one of them came down head foremost, which was very wonderful. Then, having suspended ropes from various parts of the vault, and stretched a net beneath these, an English gymnast performed thereon feats which to this day I had never seen or heard of. I will merely record here that it was not an exhibition of gymnastics, but of magic and flying. For instance, he sprang from one rope to another suspended in the air, a distance of ten cubits; and, in conclusion, threw himself in a summersault from the rope down into the net. The exhibition was thus brought to a close, and the assembly broke up.

"We went up stairs and dined at a table where all the nobles and grandees were collected. From hence the garden of the Crystal Palace, the finest garden in England, was seen. Numerous fountains, each throwing its water 75 feet high, were before us. The source of these is a high tower at the entrance end of the Palace. Crowds of people with their umbrellas over their heads, were waiting, in spite of the heavy rain, at the foot of the building, and cried hurrah! After dinner came the fireworks, which were magnificent, especially the shells, out of which burst forth stars of various colours. These concluded, we came down. They had prepared an electricity, like a telegraph wire; and the very instant that I touched it with my hand a large flight of rockets soared from the middle of the garden up into the air, and formed a beautiful sight. Then, returning, we took the hand of the wife of the Heir-Apparent and went home.

"The beggars of Europe, in lieu of soliciting alms, play musical instruments. They take any money offered to them; otherwise, they incessantly play on. In the garden at the rear of our palace-residence we have seen many pheasants, male and female, in the trees. Pigeons are numerous in Europe; and, as in Persia, pigeon-fliers fly pigeons. In Belgium especially, I saw many. Infants and sucklings are seated in small carriages and are wheeled about by hand in the streets and parks all day long; which is very pretty to see. These children go to sleep in their vehicles. I received four deer from the Duke of Sutherland, of those feeding in the park, which are of the species of the argali, but are like the stag. I have confided them to one of my suite, and I hope to bring them to Tehran, and introduce the breed.

"*Tuesday, July 1st.*—To-day, having to visit the Bank, the Tower, St. Paul's, Westminster Abbey, and the Houses of Parliament, we started after breakfast, drove through the city to the Tower, the officials of which waited on us. We went up into a very ancient turret, within which was a large glass case, with an iron railing around it. In this were several crowns of the ancient kings of England, set with choice jewels. Especially, in one crown was a large ruby of exceeding beauty. There were golden sticks (sceptres), and a few vessels of gold. Also a model of the Kūh-i-Nūr diamond in crystal; but the diamond itself, cut in London into a brilliant and set as a broach, is worn on her bosom by the Queen, as on the day when we went to Windsor to take leave of Her Majesty. It is a very fine stone. Not having the needful time we did not see the armoury, which is in this same building, but proceeded to St. Paul's. The Chief Priest was unwell and had not come; his assistant received us instead. We took a tour in the church, which is very grand and ancient. Crowds of men and women were there. The following are some of the celebrities interred there:—Lord Nelson, the Duke of Wellington.

"We then went to the State Bank, passing by the Royal Exchange, a place for the transaction of commercial business. The chief merchants of London were there in great numbers. At the gate of the Bank the governor, directors, and clerks received us. It is a large place. We went over the chamber of the archives, the council-chamber, and other rooms where the bank-notes are printed, the coins are weighed, the light coins are cut in two, by means of beautiful machines worked by steam power. We inscribed our name in a book kept for that purpose, and then went down into the vaults underground, and saw a quantity of ingots of gold and bars of silver, each golden ingot being of the value of 2,000 tūmāns of Persia (of 8*s*. 4*d*. each). About 3 or 4 crores (1,500,000*l*. to 2,000,000*l*.) of money was in that place. We then returned home. Three things seen there were very strange. First, in every machine used for printing the bank-notes, three dials were seen with hands like those of a watch, and so arranged that whatever number was printed of these notes, the dials, by means of the revolutions of their hands, kept an account of the same; each movement given to the machine caused a bank-note to come forth printed, and a hand of the dial passed from subdivision to subdivision of its face. This is to prevent the bank-notes being stolen. Secondly, the machines for weighing gold and silver coins, which are so arranged that, as fast as the coins flow down a species of gutter, they are weighed, and the light coins cast into a compartment by themselves, while those of full weight pass on to another compartment. Thirdly, a machine for cutting in two the light coins, that they may no longer pass current, but go to be reminted.

"After a while we drove to visit Gladstone, the Premier, at his abode. He had an aged wife. Both came to meet us. Giving my arm to his wife, we went up stairs into some very nice apartments, where there was a diminutive basin with jets of water—extremely pretty. The Ambassadors of Austria, Turkey, and Germany, Lord Granville —the Foreign Secretary, the wife of the Duke of

Sutherland, &c., were there; and from thence we went, after a little stay, to the Houses of Parliament.

"It is an impossibility for one to describe this building and to recount the rooms, upper rooms, and corridors thereof. They say that a fabulous sum has been spent upon it in course of time, and that it is 800 years old in part, though much added to about 10 years ago. The Regulator of the House of Lords, an old man named Clifford, walked before us, and we went from room to room. It is a very grand, solid, and imposing structure. Indeed, for the Parliament of England, so grand a palace is most fitting and becoming. We went to a large hall called the Waterloo Chamber, where were two paintings, of large dimensions and great talent, hung on the two sides. One represents the battle of Trafalgar, formerly mentioned. The other is the meeting of Wellington with Marshal Blucher, commander of the Prussians, a sharer of the battle of Waterloo. After the defeat of Napoleon they met and shook hands on horseback on the field of battle, and they congratulated each other. This is shown in the painting. We went into the Chamber of the Lords, who were assembled, in number above 100, and sat down awhile, proceeding thence, by various rooms and corridors, to the Chamber of the House of Commons. The number of members was about 350. (The diary appears to give the two numbers as the totals of the members of the two houses.) Lord Gladstone, Disraeli, and others of the Whig and Tory administrations were present. The Whigs were on one side, the Tories on the other. We were upstairs—to which a narrow passage led, and sat on a chair overlooking the assembly. A question was started on which there was a difference of opinion, and the President declared who had the majority or greater number, the lesser number being called the minority. All the members went out to be counted, and the chamber was left empty. Excepting the President, no soul remained. After a minute or two they returned, the Whigs having the majority, who are now in office. Then Lord Gladstone, the Premier, came to us and we conversed a little before going to see Westminster Abbey.

"The Abbey is close to the Houses of Parliament, and is an imposing pile, of great antiquity, and of stone. Its roof is high-pitched and of great length. Henry VII, King of England, built a beautiful chapel adjoining the Abbey, and, as it were, a royal balcony to it. It has many sculptures in the roof and walls, and the tomb of Henry himself is there. In the middle there is a large iron railing. A great number of worthies, kings, generals, and even poets, are buried in this church. Its length is 530 English feet, its height 225. King Edward the Confessor, Henry III, Henry V, Henry VII, Elizabeth, all the Sovereigns of the House of Stuart, all those of the House of Hanover, are buried here also. Of statesmen, Pitt, Fox, Sir Robert Peel, Lord Palmerston; of generals, Outram, and Lord Clyde, have their tombs in the Abbey. There is an ancient throne here, seated on which the Sovereigns of England are crowned. In it is set the stone of Jacob, on whom be peace! This is a large stone on which Jacob slept. It came to Europe from Egypt; that is, passing from one possessor to another, it became at length the property of the Kings of England. From hence we returned home.

"In the House of Parliament there is a very extensive library, containing all the ancient and modern debates of the Houses. The laws of England, &c., are also written there, in separate volumes.

"*Wednesday, July 2nd.*—After breakfast received

the Heir-Apparent of Russia, and conversed; for we are going away, and he also is going to one of the sea-ports of England to be present at the launch of a ship built there for him, and now ready. After his departure, we went to Windsor to take leave of the Queen, accompanied by the Grand-Vazīr and others of our suite. Her Majesty received us at the foot of the staircase. Taking one another by the hand, we went upstairs, and Her Majesty led me to see all the apartments of the palace, large rooms and saloons, with charming views from the windows, in the direction of London and of the country. There is a fine flower garden under the walls of the castle towards the fields. There is also a large library, where I was shown some Persian manuscripts, especially a history of India, written like a diary, and ornamented with beautiful Indian illuminations—a magnificent book. The armoury is excellent, replete with ancient arms and armour from India and elsewhere, preserved in glass cases. Vessels of gold, some enriched with precious stones; the richly jewelled throne and saddle of Tipū Sāhib (*sic*) of India; ancient arms and armour of Europe, articles sent as presents by various Sovereigns, &c., &c., &c., were in great numbers in the apartments. There was a very large vase of malachite, sent by the Emperor Nicholas of Russia; the bullet that caused Lord Nelson's death at Trafalgar, extracted from his body, and preserved in a case. In one room there were collected the yard (or mast) of the ship in which Nelson was killed, through which a cannon-ball had passed, and several of the cannon balls; and these are surrounded with a railing. Some of the Russian cannon-balls from Sebastopol, and two Russian soldier's muskets, are also placed there as samples. A bust of Nelson in stone is also placed upon a half mast (or yard) injured by a cannon-ball; and two cannons sent as presents by Runject Singh were there. In the saloons were portraits of the Sovereigns and Ministers of celebrity in the days of the first Napoleon, who formed the Holy Alliance. We then went to a table and took our seats, I, the Queen, her youngest daughter, and Prince Leopold, who again to-day had come to the station to meet me. Again he was dressed in the Scotch costume. He is a very nice prince. After taking a little fruit, we arose, and Her Majesty accompanied me to the door of a room assigned to me, and then went away. I presented my photograph (reflection) to Her Majesty as a souvenir, and the Queen gave me one of herself and one of Prince Leopold. Indeed, from my first arrival on English soil, up to this very day, Her Majesty has exercised towards us the fulness of kindness and friendship. Again we came down, and, taking Her Majesty's hand, we went to the door of the carriage, and, bidding an adieu, I got in. Her Majesty expressed a wish that her special photographer should take my likeness in the carriage, and he took several negatives. We then drove off; but shortly, turning from the direct road, we went to the residence of Her Majesty's daughter, the Princess Helena, wife of Prince Christian, one of the Princes of the House of Holstein in Germany, of which Prussia is now in possession, but to which the Prince has a claim, and may one day become its possessor. On arriving at the house, we remained a short time. The house and flower-garden are very charming. After partaking of some fruit, we drove to the mausoleum of Prince Albert, Her Majesty's husband. The distance was considerable. We passed by the side of the mausoleum of the Duchess of Kent (Duchesse de Quinte), Her Majesty's mother. On arriving at the mausoleum, we alighted and went up to the tomb. It is very imposing and in good taste, and is of stones of various colours. The sarcophagus is of stone; and an effigy of Prince Albert lying in death, of beautiful marble, is placed upon it. I laid on the tomb a nosegay which I had in my hand. I was much affected and saddened. We then drove off, being accompanied in all these visits by Prince Leopold. These parts are occupied by the private hot-houses for flowers, fruits, and vegetables, by gardens, by cow-houses and the dairy, where butter and milk are prepared for the Queen. We alighted and planted a cedar (mountain cypress) as a souvenir; thence drove to the station, bid adieu to Prince Leopold, and returned to town.

"After a little rest we drove to Madame Tussaud's Exhibition. She was a woman who has now been dead twenty years, but has left a son and grandson. She has formed a place containing the effigies in wax of ancient and modern Sovereigns, men of note, and great poets, clothed in the dress of the person and the period, whether man or woman, together with imitation jewellery, as crowns, necklaces, rings, &c.; and these effigies are arranged, some standing, others sitting, in rooms and halls, in such fashion that one cannot distinguish them from living persons. Madame Tussaud's son was ill, and her grandson was presented to me. They have made the figure of Napoleon III, dressed in his own costume, and lying on a bed at the moment of death. It is the very picture of a still living, though moribund, man. Some living ladies were seated here and there among the effigies; and it was utterly impossible for me to distinguish which were alive and which were of wax, until the former rose and walked away or smiled; then I knew they were living human beings. The effigy of Her Majesty the Queen, those of her children, and of the Ministers, were there; also those of Louis Philippe, of the Heir-Apparent of France, with his mother Eugénie. They were very beautiful. Besides the effigies of kings and magnates, there were those of some individuals — murderers or scoundrels, who had acquired an evil reputation for wickedness and satanic qualities—very striking; such as one of Orsini, who attempted the life of Napoleon III, and another of Mazzini the Italian. There is also a gallows (guillotine), by suspending a man to which, they put him to death. This they bought in France, and placed it here to show how men are there killed. They said that with this gallows-tree nearly 20,000 persons have been killed. Furthermore, there were many relics of bygone days, mostly of Napoleon I; his carriages that fell into the hands of the English after the battle of Waterloo. The very carriage used by Napoleon himself was shown; the plan of battle drawn out by Napoleon himself; the whip of his coachman used on the day of the battle; the cloak and some of the clothes of the Emperor. There were also relics of some of the ancient and modern kings and celebrities of England, &c.

"Leaving this exhibition we entered the extensive bazaar beneath it, where are sold every kind of things one can think of. We bought some glassware, &c., returned home, and went to rest.

"*Thursday, July 3rd.*—After breakfast went to the Crystal Palace by train from the Victoria Station. We passed over the roofs of the houses. Not in one place, nor in two places, but uninterruptedly we went either over the houses or through holes in the hills, and in twenty minutes reached the Crystal Palace Station, where we alighted and mounted flights of steps on foot. Crowds of men and women were there, beyond all computation. We bought some photographs, &c. The dealers in this bazaar are all women, and there are wares of all kinds. The following is the history of this Palace :—

"About twenty years ago, when the English Government established in Hyde Park an Exhibition Bazaar, which was within the town of London, and the same was closed, certain members brought it to this spot, which is out of the town, and erected it as a palace in its original form, establishing therein a permanent exhibition, erecting hotels and places of pastime for the people of London, fountains, basins of water, parks, gardens, and everything that can amuse men; so that it is now the best of all places of amusement for London, and daily, as a perpetuity, 7,000 or 8,000 persons go there to walk about and witness the spectacles; and those who have made the place derive a profit from it.

"Having made our purchases, we passed forward between the men and women, and saw several negresses (mulattoes) from the islands of Jamaica, who were very pretty, and were with their husbands, in spite of their black (dark) faces, being seated among the fair and rosy women of England. Still, with the gracefulness they possessed, they looked very coquettish.

Their complexion was of the colour of unroasted coffee. They had very nice ringlets.

"Passing on, we came to a place where a maned lion of Africa and an Indian tiger (stuffed) were fighting with each other, and a dead stag was lying beneath them. All three animals, of life size, were so formed, and so made to stand, that it was impossible not to take them for a live lion, a live tiger, and a dead stag. Their paws clenched, and the blood flowing, were as though at that moment the flesh of their bodies was fresh torn and the blood shed. So beautifully correct is the execution, that one could admire it for ten days and not be surfeited.

"We next went to see a court set up on the model of the Hamrā (red) Palace, built by the Arabs at the time of their occupation of Andalusia and Toledo, in Spain. This court is very pretty and pleasing; the plaster work and glazed-tile work is well done. A few years ago this structure was burnt, and has been restored to its original state, but is not quite finished, as the plaster work, &c., is still being done. The plaster work here is not like that of Persia; there the whole is done by hand, with great trouble; whereas here they have prepared moulds of glue with various figures, and any figure which they wish to reproduce they place its mould on a surface of plaster, and forthwith the figure is formed, and dries quickly in like manner; then, like a brick or tile, they fix this to a wall. There were four fountains and basins in the Arabian style.

"Thence we proceeded to the aquarium, and went down a few steps to a long, vaulted, underground hall, with a deliciously cool atmosphere, where we saw various kinds of marine animals and plants, as at Berlin; but at Berlin there were more kinds of fish, &c., than we saw here. We again ascended, passed through the crowds, and went up the steps over which we passed on the night of the fireworks, viewed the gardens and fountains, and passed through the grounds to see two balloons that were to ascend with people in them. We went a long way on foot, through masses of men and women, among whom were numbers of policemen. At the extremity of the gardens were two immense balloons filled with vapour and ready to ascend, in such a fashion that there was no power to restrain them. They are made of a kind of silk cloth; varnished, to give them strength. A net of rope, like a fisherman's net, was passed over each balloon, and beneath there was a basket, in which men sit, and of a size to hold two or three persons. In the first balloon a person named Smith, with another named Evenau, having seated themselves, ascended into the air, and the balloon was lost to sight. The second was taken charge of by the son of Smith, a youth, who said he had made 170 ascents with his father before that day; he also went up. On the morrow information was given that the first of the two balloons came down at a distance of ten leagues from London; the second, at one league.

"We then returned on foot to the basins of water and the fountains. The crowds were such there was no passing. By management I was enabled to inspect the whole. Returning, we mounted a carriage and drove back. The path was hilly and we went fast; but the ladies, the maidens, and the children kept pace with us, and none remained behind. Having regained the palace, we partook of some fruit, and our photograph was taken. We then left by the train, went home, rested a little, and proceeded to the Albert Hall.

The machinery was not at work, so we went to a saloon where they have collected the tobacco-pipes and huqqas, and the drinking-vessels of all nations; also silk cloths of China, Japan, and Europe, &c., ancient and modern. Having seen these, we went up stairs to examine the paintings and portraits which have been brought to the exhibition in the space of three months during which it has been open, some for sale, others for view only. We inspected the whole, but the greater number of the better ones were either sold already, or were not for sale. We selected ten or fifteen, and Smith Sāhib interpreted for me. I saw a painting of a donkey, of which I inquired the price. The President of the Exhibition, a fat man with a white beard, who knows the prices, said it was 100*l.* sterling, equivalent to 250 tūmāns of Persia. I said that a living donkey was at most worth 5*l.*, and asked how it was that the picture of one should be asked so high a price for. The President replied, 'Because it requires no expense, and eats no straw and barley.' I replied, 'True; but it carries no burden and accommodates no rider;' and we laughed heartily. It was now late and I was tired, so I went home. The Albert Hall has its own special garden, which is very beautiful.

"*Friday, July 4th.*—After breakfast went to pay a visit to the Heir-Apparent of England. The wives of the two Heirs-Apparent of Russia and England, with Prince Alfred, were also present. After a little conversation I returned home, and, after a short delay, drove to St. Thomas' Hospital, situated opposite the Houses of Parliament. The nation has constructed this hospital, which was built in the reign of Edward IV, and it is now two or three years only since it was completed. It has its estates held in mortmain; and furthermore, from that time to the present day, people collect money every year of their own free will and give it for the sustentation of the hospital; for the food and medicines of each sick person are furnished gratis. It is a very grand edifice, and there are never less than 400 or 500 patients in it—men, and women, young and old. Dr. Tholozan also was present. The President of the Board of Health of London (Medical Officer of the Local Government Board), named Simon, with the chief medical men and surgeons of London, were there also. Every little child had a bed to himself, and clean bed-clothes; and each, to amuse him, had playthings and many pretty objects that have been collected. There were very many women acting as attendants.

We went next to a men's ward. In spite of their being invalids they called out hurrah. In the lower story they have appliances by which, having placed a patient on a bed, they lift him to the upper wards without his having to use any exertion. Her Majesty laid the foundation stone of the present building.

"I then went to the house of Lord (the Duke of) Argyll, Secretary for India, which is at a distance. We went through Hyde Park, &c. The wife of the Secretary for India, who is the sister of the Duke of Sutherland, and a woman in years, with the daughter of Her Majesty, who is the wife of the Secretary's son, came to meet me; and, taking their hands, I went for a little turn in the garden, thence to a room where a table was spread, and where I partook of some fruit. The Duke of Sutherland was also there. We then returned to the garden and sat awhile in a tent pitched there. A Scotchman in Scotch garb came and piped, while another, similarly dressed, danced a Scotch dance. He placed four swords upon a round board, and danced around these swords. A man of the name of Viteston (Wheatstone) has invented a variety of telegraph which enables people to converse with one another, say, between London and Tehran, and which prints the message on paper, so that it may be easily read off. They had arranged one of these in the garden, and we went to see it. We then took leave and drove to Hyde Park, dismounted, and went to inspect the structure which Her Majesty has erected in memory of (Prince) Albert, her consort. It is entirely of stone, with very handsome sculptures, in which they have collected and arranged the effigies, in stone, of the notabilities and poets and painters of the world, and others; the reason being that (Prince) Albert himself was a man of science and of art. The crowds hindered me from examining the details, so I drove home; and, in the evening, went to Drurelam (Drury Lane) Theatre, through crowds collected in the streets. The Heir-Apparent of England was there, and received me. Taking his hand we went up to a box near the stage. His son Alfred (*sic*) also came. An opera and ballet were performed, the singing and dancing being good, and the dancers being handsome and beautifully attired. This theatre has five tiers of balconies, rather small, but pretty. There was a young female singer named Nelson (*sic*) from Sweden. The Heir-Apparent had her brought up, and chatted with her awhile. She is very chatty and witty. All the year round she goes to the theatres of Peter(sburg), America, &c., and makes a large income. She has taken as her husband a Frenchman of the name of Gousseau.

"Returning thence, we called at the Palace of St. James, built in the olden time, so that the Court of England is still named the Court of St. James. Formerly the Queen used to hold her Court there; but since the demise of her consort she has never gone there, and at present the mother of the Duke of Cambridge is held to reside at this Palace. From thence went home. Yesterday one of our suite went over to Paris to settle about our journey-stations, and the like. If I were to entertain the wish to describe as they deserve the details of the city of London, or of all England, I should have to write an immense volume of English history. For a stay of eighteen days in London, more than this has not been written. In justice, I can only add that the conduct of the English, as everything else of theirs, is well ordered, well regulated, and excellent. In point of prosperity, of wealth, of commerce, of art, of industry, and of indolent ease and pleasure, they are the chief of all nations.

"*Saturday, July 5th.*—Having to proceed to-day to the port of Cherbourg in France, I rose early. During the eighteen days of my stay in London, the weather has been cloudy. Many purchases have also been made here.

"The Heir-Apparent of England, the Foreign Secretary Lord Granville, Lord Sydney, Prince Alfred, Prince Arthur, and others, having arrived, we mounted a carriage and drove to the station. Large crowds had assembled in the deepest concern. It was evident that the English people were at heart sorely grieved at our departure.

"Arrived at the Victoria Station, the Heir-Apparent took leave; but Prince Alfred and Prince Arthur, with the Grand-Vazīr, took seats in our carriage. We left behind in London, to study, the son of the Hakīmu-'l-Mamālik. We reached Portsmouth in less than three hours, having passed on the road the towns of Mitcham, Epsom, Dorking, Horsham, Arundel, and Chichester. The forts and ships saluted. We were received by Admiral Beauchamp Seymour, the Admiral in command of the station, and were conducted on board a French ship, formerly named 'L'Aigle,' having been built for Napoleon III, and since the establishment of the Republic renamed 'Rapide.' We shortly began our voyage. The most direct, most pleasant, and proper route is from Dover in England to Calais in France, the sea-passage there occupying only an hour and a half, while that from Portsmouth to Cherbourg takes eight hours. Our suite were embarked in another vessel, which followed behind us, while four English men-of-war kept to right and left of us as an escort of honour. In mid-channel eight sail of French men-of-war met us, and fired a salute. The English men-of-war saluted also, consigned us to the French, and returned. We reached Cherbourg about sun-down. The ships there illuminated."

The following morning we landed under a beautiful triumphal arch, and were received by all the chiefs and officers of the army, navy, and civil Government. In driving to the station we were struck with the diminutiveness of stature and the leanness of the French men and women, who are not like the inhabitants of Russia, Germany, and England, but much more resemble easterns. Cherbourg could not easily be taken by force.

We passed through Normandy, a fine fertile country, abounding in cattle. Here also most of the common trees of Persia were seen. The country is hilly; its apples are famous. Passed by Caen, and went through a tunnel a league in length—very suffocating. Arrived at Paris towards evening, and was received at Passy by Marshal MacMahon, the Duc de Broglie, &c., who conducted me, through lines of infantry, cavalry, and gens-d'armes, to the Palace of the Corps Législatif, assigned for my residence. At the Arc de Triomphe we were received by M. Duval and the city authorities, and answered the address there made by them to us. At the entrance to our residence another discourse was pronounced by M. Buffet, President of the Assembly, and also answered by us. We were shown to our rooms, and they had prepared for my use the bedstead on which the first Napoleon used to sleep after his marriage with Marie Louise.

To-day I have witnessed a strange demeanour on the part of the French. In the first place they are still mourning the German war. Old and young, they are all gloomy and downcast. The women are dressed, and the men also, in mourning, very plain, very few ornaments. Some of the men, instead of shouting "Vive le Maréchal," called out "Vive le Chah de Perse." One night also, as I was taking a walk, I heard one of them say "May his reign and rule endure!" From these it is clear that a great change has come over the French, and they are desirous of a monarch. They are of three parties: one wishes for the son of Napoleon, another for the son of Louis Philippe, and the third for Henri Cinq. The Republicans, too, are very strong, but they are not of one mind; those of the Rouge party wish for a real republic, while the Moderates wish for a republic with monarchical institutions without a monarch; and other opinions also are entertained. It is difficult to carry on a Government under such circumstances, and complications must arise out of them, unless they unite in desiring either a monarchy or a republic. When united, France is the strongest of nations, and all must take her into consideration; but, with these dissensions, it is far from likely she should preserve order. The commonality of Paris do whatever they chose; the Government has not the power to check them. The Commune burnt down the Palace of the Tuileries, the finest palace in the world. Thank God the Louvre was saved, though adjoining it. They also burnt the Hôtel-de-Ville and the Palace of the Légion d'Honneur; they overthrew the Colonne de (la place) Vendôme, which the first Napoleon had cast out of the materials of cannon taken from the enemy, and on the top of which he had placed his own statue, figuring the whole of his wars around it.

Paris is a beautiful city, and the prevalence of sunshine there is like we have it in Persia. At night it is lighted throughout with gas. Carriages are numerous, and people enjoy themselves at the cafés. The Seine is not like the Thames: it is narrow and shallow, so that large ships cannot navigate it.

Next day drove to the Jardin d'Acclimatisation, and among other animals saw some kangaroos from Australia, something like a jerboa; it cannot walk, but jumps, its fore-feet being very short, and its hind-legs very large; it is about the size of a jackal. The female has a pouch under its abdomen in which its young live for a time after birth. Women and children rode about in howdahs on two elephants; and a droshka, with people in it, was drawn by a large ostrich.

I then went to the aquarium, which is very small and poor. From thence drove to the Bois de Boulogne, and visited an island in the lake, where the marks of cannon-shot and bullets were thick on the trees. Drove about; went home; dined; drove about by night. "There is no possibility to write up my diary properly with all this gadding; but I write succinctly what is most important."

One day the foreign Representatives were received in audience, as there are here either an Ambassador, a Minister, or a Chargé d'Affaires from every Government, even from Japan and the Island of Hayti. The Ambassadors are—Chigi, Papal Nuncio; Lord Lyons, of England; Olosaga, of Spain; Prince Orloff, of Russia, who lost his left eye at the siege of Silistria in the days of the Crimean war, and received other wounds from sabre-cuts, &c.; he wore a black bandage over his injured eye; Appony, of Austria. Several French Diplomatists, who had been in Persia, came also; "they were all fatter and younger."

One day I went to see the palace and gardens of Versailles, and the weather was very sultry. The palace is the chief building in Europe for its statuary, paintings, and architecture. Marshal MacMahon received me, and accompanied me over the gardens, and presented his wife, son, and daughters. "In one place there was an artificial mountain with a waterfall, and under the waterfall were several marble statues, one being that of Apollo, the god of manly beauty, who is ornamenting himself, while the others hold his mirror, his ornaments, flowers, &c. It is a most beautiful group. I expressed a wish to go up near to the statues under the waterfall. The Marshal and another general said it would be very difficult, as the path was precipitous, steep, and rocky. I said I would go; I got down out of the carriage, and went up. The path was disagreeable; but it had no difficulty for me, accustomed as I am to climb much worse paths in Persia in pursuit of the chase. When I had reached the statues the general followed; but he had a tumble, bemudded all his clothes, and bent or broke his sword. The Marshal came up also, but with great difficulty and with the assistance of several others. This manner of getting up casts no slur upon the pluck and determination of a marshal and a general of France."

Within the palace Marshal Canrobert and the Comte de Palikao were presented. The former greatly distinguished himself in the Crimea, but suffered much tribulation through being one of the prisoners of Metz, and a subordinate of Bazaine. The latter said he was writing a history of the campaign in China. I also met two sons of Louis Philippe, the Duc d'Aumale, and the

Prince de Joinville, both men of ability, but the latter rather deaf. The Comte de Paris was not there.

Visited the bedchamber of Louis Quatorze, with his bedstead and bedclothes; and there dined with the Marshal and a large company of officials, the Grand-Vazir and our Princes being also at table. In the evening the palace and gardens were illuminated, and fireworks were exhibited. We then drove home by way of St. Cloud, the palace of which was burnt in the German war, though its parks and drives are intact.

One day we went to the Invalides, where is the tomb of the first Napoleon, those of his brothers and marshals, as well as those of more ancient worthies of the times of Louis XIV. The old wounded veterans, some with one leg, one arm, or none, and some with one eye, were drawn out and received us with military honours, we returning their salute. General Martinprai, the Governor, received us—a very old man and palsied, who had been Governor of Algeria and Chief of the Staff in the wars of Italy and the Crimea. We went into the chapel and saw a beautiful altar erected by Louis Philippe, behind which is the tomb of the first Napoleon, whose remains were

brought from St. Helena by that king and
entombed here. The stone (sarcophagus) that
covers the tomb, of a pea-green colour, was brought
from the Island of Corsica; and the lid, a beautiful
stone from Siberia of a reddish tinge, was a
present from the Emperor Nicholas of Russia.
In this establishment I saw several old soldiers
who were at the battles of Waterloo, Friedland,
and Jena, being still robust; as Captain Duchemin,
Chassy, Branche. Near the tomb, in a glass case,
are deposited the hat of Napoleon and the sword
which he wore at Austerlitz. "I lifted them
both so as to have in my hand such relics of
so great a Sovereign and general. The hat was
quite plain; the sword was straight, and has
rusted in its sheath, so that it cannot be drawn.
I replaced them with great veneration." Of the
590 inmates of the establishment, 35 had served
under the first Napoleon. There are flags in it
taken from the enemy dating from the time of
Louis XIV, who built the place in A.D. 1670,
and others of later times; forty-six such flags
are arranged round the tomb of Napoleon, taken
by him, and in the chapel are 245 others.

M. Crémieux was presented to me,—a little
old man and a Jew, but a great orator, who always

opposed the late Emperor, and is in opposition in the present Assembly. M. Rothschild, another Jew and possessing a very large fortune, was also presented. "In conversation he greatly upheld the Jews; he mentioned the Jews of Persia, entreating quiet and security for them. I made answer: 'I have heard that you and your brothers possess 500,000,000*l.* (1,000 crores) of money; and it appears to me that the best thing you can do is to give 50 crores to some state, great or small, and purchase a territory to which you could bring the Jews of the whole world, and become their head; they would then live in peace and safety, and not be scattered and lost.' We laughed heartily, but he made no reply. I gave him my assurance that I protect all strangers in Persia."

M. Lesseps, who, by aid of a great company, has united the Mediterranean and Red Seas, so that India, Persia, China, &c., are now, for commercial purposes, 2,000 leagues nearer to Europe than before, came also to our presence with his son, a youth. "He now has a new project in his head—to construct a railway from Orenbourg in Russia to Samarkand, and thence to Peshawur in British India; but this is a project very distant and round about."

M. Nadar, a photographer of merit in Paris, was also presented, and took my likeness. "He has formerly ascended often in balloons; but has now renounced that whim, and exercises photography." M. Tardieu, "M. Larrey, son of Larrey, the surgeon to the first Napoleon, and himself a surgeon of repute, and M. Cloquet, uncle to the Cloquet who was chief physician to the late Sovereign (my father), and physician to myself, but who met his death by drinking one night in mistake some tincture of cantharides instead of wine," presented their respects too.

Another day I drove to Longchamps to review the troops. Marshal MacMahon, the Duc de Nemours, General Ladmirault, &c., met me on horseback in the Bois de Boulogne, where I also mounted one of my chargers. We first reviewed about 1,000 cavalry, partly cuirassiers, partly hussars; and then about 120 battalions of infantry, of about 400 to 500 men each, the rest being absent on furlough. There were 300 pieces of artillery, "all horsed." They saluted us in the military fashion by drooping their colours, &c., and we returned their salute. We were then shown to a seat on a stand where many persons of distinction and many beautiful ladies were assembled, while other stands were occupied by members of the Assembly and by the foreign Representatives. The march past occupied nearly three hours, as altogether there were about 80,000 troops of all arms present, who afforded a magnificent spectacle. "After all those defeats and ruin to France, I had not anticipated such an array and such discipline. They were beautifully dressed; they were all armed with Chassepot rifles of the old pattern, and the artillery the same as those with which they fought the Germans."

Another day I went with the Marshal to witness the horse-races at Longchamps. The heats were named after the provinces of Persia, such as Ispahan, Shiraz, &c. The course is short, and the horses all come in together, with only a head or a head and neck, &c., difference. "Our Persian mode of racing is much better, and makes more show. Our course is half a league round, and six rounds, *i.e.*, three leagues, and sometimes seven rounds, make one heat. When a horse wins there, he has done something worth seeing. Here, where the utmost extent of the course is only half a league, the horse cannot show his worth." Another kind of race was a hurdle-race. They set up several wooden barriers, about a cubit high, and the horses had to leap over these. This was better.

Returning, I alighted at the Arc de Triomphe, and ascended to the top, with my suite, by 285 steps, narrow and winding, difficult to mount. "I got up without stopping for breath, but my companions mounted slowly." The view of all Paris thence is beautiful; but the scene created by the crowds of carriages returning from Longchamps was wonderful. Seven lines of carriages occupied the road from the Bois de Boulogne to the other end of the Champs Élysées; and when we remounted our carriage it was impossible to get through the crowd, so that we had great trouble in reaching home.

In the evening the Marshal came to conduct us to see the illuminations and fireworks. From our residence onwards the crowds were enormous, so that I must have seen half a million of men and women. All cried out, "Vive le Chah de Perse." They also praised the Marshal, and said, "Vive la France." Timber pavilions had been put up for our accommodation at the Trocadero, also for the public functionaries, foreign Representatives, &c. The spectacle was superb, but the weather was untoward, with high wind and some rain.

Another evening we went to the Cirque, "which is a place of amusement like a theatre, but better." That evening the seats were paid for at the rate of even 30 and 50 tūmāns each. There were fifty or sixty horses, very handsome, but of colours such as I had never seen. There were speckled horses that must have been worth 500 to 1,000 tūmāns. They are so well trained and taught that they obey every signal and understand every word said to them. The performers, women, men, and children, utterly astounded me by their feats.

From thence proceeded to the Louvre, where all the savans and scientific men of Paris were assembled. The Vazīr of Sciences, a very fat and tall man, named Batbie, was there. Cuirassiers with torches in their hands preceded us; the learned men walked on each side in two rows, and the Vazīr kept near me; and so we went about viewing the ancient and modern statues there collected. Afterwards we went home.

One day I visited the Panorama, and saw downstairs a scene of the effects of the bombardment in a street, with the men, women, and children fleeing from their houses; and upstairs the general view of Paris besieged by the Germans, and the bombardment going on. Both were wonderfully lifelike. I also visited the church of Notre Dame, which is of stone and is 500 or 600 years old. Every part was beautiful. I was taken to see the "Treasury," where were vessels of gold, gilt, and silver. There I saw the Chief Priest and conversed with him. "Especially I inquired of him : ' What is your belief concerning the Holy Jesus (on whom be peace !) ? Did he ever drink wine or not ?' With one accord the priests, as though I had asked a strange question, answered all together : ' Undoubtedly he did drink it; that is as nothing; he himself also made wine.' Then I asked : ' Did he drink little or much ?' They all said : ' Much.' "

I then proceeded to the École-des-Mines, where I saw specimens of all the ores of the world, from gold to coal, especially some beautiful emeralds from New Grenada, still fixed in their stony matrix, as dug up. Also others from Siberia and elsewhere, large, but of low quality. Of course, to learn properly all about these would take a long time, whereas I could give but a few minutes to the survey. On an upper floor were the fossils—bones of animals from the days before Noah's flood, "and since then"; also fossilized animals. The study of these is a science of itself.

On sundry occasions I visited the Palais du Luxembourg, assigned for the use of the Senate by Napoleon, but now used instead of the burnt Hôtel-de-Ville for the offices of the city; the Panthéon, now under repairs for the injuries sustained during the late troubles; St. Sulpice, and the Madeleine. One evening I went to the Palais Royal, surveyed all the shops, and made some purchases. On another occasion went to the Mint, where silver only is coined now, "so much gold having been paid over to Prussia." A pair of dies had been prepared, with Persian inscriptions commemorative of my visit; and in my presence they struck off therewith three large medals, one of gold, another of silver, and a third of copper, which were presented to me as a souvenir. From thence I went on board a small steamer and ascended the Seine to its confluence with the Marne, and then returned. The banks of the river have no beauty, and its water is of small volume and very shallow. At a short distance from the city, the houses, on both banks, are very poor, being inhabited by peasants. I noticed the laundries and baths built of wood in the midst of the stream. In these baths there is a large room through which the water flows, and here the people bathe and wash themselves. The laundries are on the same principle, and all the clothes-washers are women (being all men in the east, except in private houses). There are also warm baths, heated by steam, within these establishments, "where one can really cleanse himself."

I visited the manufactory called Les Gobelins, the tapestries of which are sold at extravagant prices, but which are so beautifully wrought as to be hung in the palaces of kings for ornament like pictures. "Their defect is that the colours fade in the light, whereas Persian carpets do not easily lose their beauty."

From thence drove to the Louvre, passing by many buildings burnt down by the Commune, and by the Place de la Bastille, with its column of bronze surmounted with the figure of an angel of gilt brass, erected by Louis Philippe. The Louvre contains, among its many wonders of ancient and modern art and antiquities, an armbone of Charlemagne, "who was Emperor of Firangistān (Europe)." His sword and sceptre were also seen. But to study and understand all that is here would take a lifetime.

Passing thence into the garden of the Tuileries, I examined the ruins of this celebrated palace, burnt, with all its contents, by the Commune. To restore it, if even possible, would require an outlay of 100 crores of tūmāns (25,000,000*l.*). I walked in the gardens, now much neglected, and then drove home. I did not see the new opera-house, begun by the late Emperor, and still unfinished, requiring another million sterling to complete it. I went to visit the porcelain manufactory of Sèvres, about to be transferred to another site. I found that nothing could be purchased of the articles shown, as the establishment belongs to the State. Two large vases and two sets of tea-things, each in its own casket, of very magnificent workmanship, were presented to me as a souvenir.

On one occasion I went to Versailles to witness a sitting of the Assembly; was met by the President, conducted through a gallery adorned with marble statues of former kings and notables, and introduced into the hall of the Assembly, where 700 deputies were met together, and large numbers of spectators, men and women, were seated in the upper tiers. It was formerly the theatre of the palace. On the question under discussion several generals, &c., spoke, *e.g.*, General Noisel, whose voice was treble and weak, so that no one could hear what he said, and the Left were incessant in demanding that he should speak louder. It was a curious wrangle, the Vice-President in the chair continually ringing a little bell to signify that they should be silent. It is difficult for one to speak in such an Assembly. The sight was remarkable, and we remained there about an hour; after which I went over the apartments of the palace with Marshal MacMahon and M. Buffet, and among other wonders of art saw the statue of Jeanne d'Arc, the work of the Princess Marie, daughter of Louis Philippe, who died young and unmarried.

At another time I went to the Jardin des Plantes, and was received by the Director, M. Blanchard, of whose life seventy-five years had passed away. Here they rear all kinds of beautiful flowers and medicinal plants; here are professors of botany, always investigating and teaching the properties and virtues of every plant that grows, and rearing in hot-houses the growths of tropical climates. In the grounds devoted to animals, I saw some which I had not noticed elsewhere: the cassowary, a kind of ostrich from Australia; the tapir, from South America, a beast like a rhinoceros, but smaller; the jaguar, a kind of carnivorous brute between a tiger and panther, and **very savage**. There were two new-born panther cubs, very pretty. Elsewhere I had not seen a museum of zoology; but here I went over an extensive collection of quadrupeds, fishes, snakes, crabs, crocodiles, tortoises, and flying-creatures. It was a world of wonders. From the smallest fish to the crocodile, everything was so arranged that no one could judge whether they were alive or dead; and so of the birds, from the smallest humming-bird of America to the ostrich; all the known birds of the world are there collected, male and female, with their eggs and nests arranged in the same way as the living birds do for themselves. In an apartment where the eggs of all birds are collected, I saw four of the size of large melons, said to belong to a species of bird no longer extant. They have been found by travellers in Africa and America. These eggs were lifted up, and I found them very heavy. By analogy, the chick that would come alive out of one of those eggs would be of the size of a very large domestic cock. The Rukh and Simurg, of which we read in books, must have come out of such eggs. One of them is worth 1,000 tumans. There was one kind of monkey of the size of a horse, another as small as a mouse. A pair of gorillas, male and female, from Africa, were as large as tigers and of twice the stature of man, or even more. "Not one hair's breadth have these creatures been increased or diminished in size by art to deceive people; but, large or small, everything in that museum is a real animal, the creation of the Lord of the Universe, collected by the Franks with great exertions and at great expense, brought together from the remotest parts of the earth to promote the interests of science, to increase the habit of observation, and to exhibit the power of the Lord, as shown in the production of these wonderful works of his hands, equal care being taken to preserve them. Truly have they incurred great trouble. One should sit here for five months and contemplate these dead animals, bones, and birds, to understand something of them. What can I learn in a short quarter of an hour? I descended, and though I had no time to spare, I again went round and surveyed the whole of the live animals in their cages. The Director, a man of seventy-five, or perhaps even eighty, accompanied me about everywhere, at least a league; although I repeatedly begged him to leave, he would again return to me. He said that never in his life had he drunk intoxicating liquors, and had always dissuaded others from their use." The megatherium is an antediluvian animal of the same class as the elephant, but larger and without a trunk; its bones have been collected and deposited in the museum.

Paris has many theatres. I went one night to the largest, where all the French magnates and foreigners of distinction were present. There was beautiful singing and dancing, especially in a submarine scene, when the sea-nymphs danced. I also went one night to the Élysée, to an evening reception of all those magnates with their wives; the gardens were illuminated, and there were fireworks. The garden was also lighted up with the electric light from the roof of the palace; it was like moonlight. Those who walked about in this artificial light had a peculiar appearance.

Another evening the Duc de Broglie gave a reception in my honour at the Foreign Office, which had been closed until this occasion ever since the departure of the Ministry to Versailles after the German war.

On my visit to Vincennes, much improved by the late Emperor, I drove out through one of the gates of Paris, which are not like those of Persian cities. They have no real gates, but iron railings.

I dismounted and went on foot to examine the ditch and wall of the enceinte. The wall, which is really the scarp of the ditch, is nine cubits high, with one cubit of earth above this—ten cubits in all—surmounted with a coping of large cut stones. The angles also are formed of large cut stones, but the rest is of small stones. The counterscarp of the ditch is not very high, and is sloping, so that one can walk down into the ditch, which is ten cubits broad. This wall and ditch go all round Paris, and were constructed thirty years since by Louis Philippe. On my return home by the Boulevard Dumesmil, I was stopped in a street by a large concourse of people, and it proved to be the Sisters of Charity, who had been apprized of my coming that way; and I was requested by a priest, in excellent Persian, to go and visit their school for orphans. He had been for some years a teacher in a Roman Catholic school at Urmiyya, in Āzarbāyjān, Persia. The Sisters dress in black, with a very peculiar head-dress, resembling the ears of an elephant. The school contains six classes, and the building is of six stories, one to each class. The scholars are from three to twenty years of age, boys and girls, and are 1,000 in number. They learn mathematics, geography, languages, sewing, embroidery, &c. The girls make beautiful artificial flowers, a bouquet of which they presented to me as a souvenir. About 400 little ones of four years old, sang a hymn in my honour by heart, which their teacher, an old religious woman, had composed for them. Older girls sang another also. I was pleased with their manners and with the arrangements.

I went to the Cirque a second time, and saw some wonderful feats performed by the horses. Furthermore, a sculptor came to our residence and prepared a model of our person in clay, as is the rule in that art. They then mould a second in plaster, and lastly cut it out of marble. According to what he promised, the marble figure will be sent to Tehran in about four months' time.

There are places of amusement in Paris called "Cafés Chantants," where some of my suite were vastly entertained with singers, actors, gymnasts, and the like, but I did not myself see them. There are many hotels, the best of all being the "Grand Hôtel," which is like a royal palace, and everything one wishes for is supplied there in the way of eating and drinking. The "Jardin Mabille" is a place open every night, the price of admission to which is 5s., and something like 2,000 visitors is the usual number admitted. It has walks, basins, and fountains, an artificial mountain and cascade, &c., while in the middle is a pavilion for musicians. There is also a café, and sundry handsome rooms well lighted up. Beautiful women of every kind are great frequenters of this place. There is a similar establishment in London, but we saw neither.

In Europe there is a wonderful breed of horses, the heads and legs and hoofs of which are like those of elephants. They are used for the draught of heavy loads. I saw great numbers of them harnessed to carts and waggons in Germany, in England, and in France.

A custom prevails, also, of dressing the various members of each family alike. Thus, suppose a case of four sisters; you see them all four attired in dresses of the same shape, material, and colour. It has a very pretty effect.

Saturday, July 19*th*.—Quitted Paris and went to Dijon, chief town of the Côte d'Or, a part of Burgundy, famous for its grapes and its wines, which are sent to every part of the world. The vineyards, from their immense extent, make one wonder where all the grapes can be used. They prepare an excellent mustard here. The day following proceeded to Geneva, the latter part of the road being mountainous, with the river Rhone on our right hand. We passed through many tunnels, one being of great length. Snow became visible on the mountains. The Alps, Mont Blanc, the peaks of the great chain of Savoy and Italy, came in view. The gentlemen in attendance on us since we landed at Cherbourg here took leave and returned, as the territory of France was now left behind. The crowd in the streets from the station to the Hôtel-de-Berg, where we put up, was so dense that I every moment feared some one would be crushed to death. The police could do nothing; the President of the Republic and of the Assembly were both with me in the carriage, and with great patience and good management we at length struggled through, amid the screams of children, the shrieks of maidens, and the crush of all. As everywhere else in Europe, this Hôtel de Berg, built on the bank of the Rhone, is one of the grandest buildings in the town, and resembles a kingly palace. The water of the Rhone is very sweet and wholesome from its clearness; its colour is cerulean. The city, built on both sides of the river, has many fine buildings and bridges; its colleges, its manufactories of watches and musical boxes, are famous. All the organs and musical snuff-boxes, all the singing nightingales and crowing cocks that play by clockwork, are made here. I and my suite were here all lodged in the hotel, because in Switzerland there is no king and no regal palaces, the mode of government being quite different. All foreign Sovereigns who visit Switzerland lodge in hotels as we did. The Alps and Mont Blanc were seen from our windows. "There was much snow, but Mount Damāwand in Persia is much higher and much more beautiful than these."

[*Note*.—Black's Atlas of 1856, gives the height of Mont Blanc as 15,781 feet; that of "Demawand" at 15,000 feet; of Kazbek, 15,345 feet; and of Elburz, 17,796 feet—both these latter being in the Caucasus. Mr. Grove's letter in to-day's "Times" (26th August, 1874), gives an altitude of 18,500 feet to Elburz. Mr. Grove, however, places the Caucasus in Europe, and dethrones Mont Blanc from its supremacy as the highest in our quarter of the globe, raising Elburz to its vacated pre-eminence. General Monteith, in the map to his "Kars and Erzeroum," published in 1856, gives the same height to Elburz, 18,514 feet, but assigns to Kazbek an altitude of 16,518 feet.—J. W. R.]

On the following day we made a tour of the

Lake of Geneva on a steamer. At a short distance from the town, on our right hand, Savoy began, which was ceded to France by Italy when the late Emperor Napoleon, after the battles of Magenta and Solferino, obtained the cession of Lombardy by Austria to Italy. Savoy is not nearly so prosperous and populous as the Swiss districts on the north shores of the lake. At Vevay we were invited to dine by the President, and met the King of Holland, then travelling in those parts. On our return along the Swiss shores I observed that here too the vine is cultivated to the tops of the hills, wherever practicable.

Again, on the following day, I drove a certain distance into Savoy by a road that ended at an inn, near which I and some of my suite mounted my horses and others procured on the spot, as I wished to reach the summit of the hill behind the inn. There was no road; but I managed to make my way through scrub and scattered trees till I reached the top. The lake was then before me like a map, and the Alps like a panorama. The heat was very great; we, therefore, took shelter in a thicket and rested a while. Remounting our horses, we descended to the inn, where we found no refreshments other than iced water, as large numbers of travellers and of inhabitants from neighbouring places had assembled. Rested awhile in the small garden of the inn, washed my hands and face, and then gave audience to the local authorities, who made a speech as though I had arrived in Paris. Our return journey down hill to Geneva was very slow, so that it was dark before I got home.

The day after, being invited to breakfast at the Hôtel de la Paix with the Swiss Government, I there received the various Presidents, and also the Prussian and Italian Envoys to Switzerland, and the Swiss Envoy to France. The breakfast was very long and tedious. The inhabitants presented me with an enamelled gold box containing a watch and a crowing cock; also a rifle, with a thousand balls, as used by the Swiss troops. Later in the day went with the same company to visit various establishments in the town. At one I witnessed some experiments in electricity; but as the windows had to be closed and the room darkened, it was hot and oppressive. At another, an exhibition of works by Swiss painters, I purchased six or seven good pictures, and examined a large map in relief of all Switzerland, to the construction of which General Dufour had devoted several years; it was beautiful, exhibiting as it did every village, every stream, and every valley. I had never seen anything like it previously. In the afternoon drove out to dine with M. Faver, a rich Swiss gentleman, at his country house on the lake, and on my way passed the villa of M. Rothschild. The scenery was beautiful. Returning early, I passed a very uncomfortable night, by reason of the unceasing roll of carriages, the roar of thunder, the pelting of rain, the chiming of clocks, and the ringing of the bells in the hotel. (Here follows a short outline of the political constitution of Switzerland.)

Thursday, July 24th.—Left Geneva for Turin, the ancient capital of the Kingdom of Sardinia and Piedmont, which has now become the Kingdom of United Italy by the successive annexations of Lombardy and Venice, Naples and Sicily, and ultimately of Rome, the former capital of the Cæsars, and later the seat of the Popes, who are the heads of the Catholics, but who, in these days of the actual Pope, have been deprived of all political sway. Our road went through Savoy and its capital, Chambery, to Modane, the last French station on this line of railway. We passed through the wildest and most magnificent scenery, over great rivers, and wide, deep valleys, through which the line, with its wondrous iron bridges, has been carried at great expense and with consummate skill. At Modane the officers deputed by the King of Italy to attend us were presented, "though the frontier of the two realms is in the middle of the hole made through Mont Cenis," this hole having been pierced half way by each of the two States. It is about two leagues and a half long, and we were twenty-eight minutes passing through it. I first shut all my windows, to exclude the smoke; then I opened one or two to get a little air. At times a strange sound would come, as though a dragon were passing at speed; sometimes through the utter darkness another engine would come in sight and again be lost to view; at intervals a lamp and a guard of the line were seen, though I know not how those men manage to live in such a place, which took twenty years to pierce. Emerging at length, we passed through two other tunnels of great length, and many minor ones, perhaps eighty in all, in a country of mountains, snows, and waterfalls, precipices, valleys, and torrents. These, uniting, ultimately form the Po, which runs into the Adriatic. The valley widens into a plain full of trees before Turin is reached, and we did not arrive at the station until darkness had fallen around. Here we were received by His Majesty the King of Italy, Prince Humbert, Prince Amadeo, Prince Carignano, the Ministers, and others. The King conducted me to the palace, showed me to my apartments, through rooms and corridors richly furnished, and then took leave. Shortly after, I went to His Majesty's apartments in return, and after a little converse retired.

The air of Turin is very sultry. "The King was out in the mountains on a hunting expedition and living in tents, but had come into the city to receive me. He hunts summer and winter, and has no wish to live in town, as he told me himself." ("It is whispered that the King of Italy prefers shooting in Piedmont to all the pleasures of a palace."—"Times" leader, 27th August, 1874. The present paragraph was translated by me on the 26th.—J. W. R.) He is about sixty years of age, but hale and strong, with no appearance of decrepitude. Besides his sons he has two daughters, one married to the King of Portugal, the other to Prince Napoleon. Outside the town is a high hill with a chapel on its summit, where are the tombs of the King's ancestors. Within the town the Jews are now building a large synagogue.

Next day, after inspecting with the King the armoury of the palace, and seeing many objects of interest, we assisted at a state banquet in the evening. I observed that neither His Majesty, nor his cousin, Prince Carignano, ate anything. Inquiring the reason, the King told me that he ate at midnight only, and immediately went to bed. This was also the Prince's habit, and he said he never drank wine, preferring iced water. In the course of the day His Majesty had sent me as souvenirs many things of great value, such as cameos, mosaics, fowling-pieces, a portrait of himself, marble models of buildings, bronze statues, &c.; and to my Grand-Vazīr and Princes he gave the insignia of orders. At night we went to the theatre of the palace.

The day following, among other things, I went to see the King's private collection of wild beasts, and here, for the first time, saw an ounce (?), and a kind of malignant baboon called a "mandrill," with a yellow beard, red nose, and blue cheeks with grooves. A cheetah I had seen before; an ounce, never. On my return I was saved the fatigue of mounting many stairs to my apartments, and was luxuriously hoisted up instead, sitting at my ease in a kind of chair like the inside of a carriage.

The King formerly had married a wife in the usual ceremonious manner of state, but she has been dead some time, and he has not taken to himself another state wife. Instead thereof he has, like myself, taken a woman informally. This woman was not at Turin, but had gone to the seaside to take baths. I had sent her a souvenir of some jewels, and she sent me her photograph. The King told me she had been his companion in all his wars, and accompanies him in all his hunting expeditions, and hunts also. He has a son by her, who is a cavalry officer; also a daughter, whom he had given in marriage to a Colonel in the army, now dead, so that she is a widow.

The next morning, I being about to start for Milan, His Majesty came to see me with Prince Amadeo, and told me that his eldest son, who set out yesterday for his country house in order to be there ready to receive me, had shot a piece of game of some kind, which was now in the palace, and wished me to see it, and say whether game of that species is met with in Persia. On inspecting it I found it was of the same kind that I had seen in such numbers in the parks in England, a kind of deer. We then went together to the station, where His Majesty took leave; and I mounted in an Austrian train of which all the carriages communicated with one another, as was the case with the one in which I travelled in Russia.

The country was, where not mountainous, very populous, well cultivated, and fertile. "The more general produce was maize, which was just ripe. The difference between this and that of Persia is that this is much taller; and also that, although the (fruit of the) middle of the stems is the same as in Persia, and is eaten, the summits of the stems are like ears of wheat, and pendulous; these also are made into flour and used as food, so that two sources of aliment come from each stem." The wheat and barley were already harvested. About Milan I observed extensive plantations of mulberry-trees for silkworms. The silk of Italy is famous for its excellent quality; but for some years it has not done well.

Our road passed by the village of Magenta, in the fields of which was fought the battle of that name, where the Austrians were totally defeated and put to rout by the French and Italians united. I saw the tall column erected by Napoleon III in memory of the victory and of the killed on the side of the French.

Arrived at Milan; the station at which, constructed while the Austrians held sway there, was the largest and most beautiful I had yet seen. The Heir-Apparent, who is the Governor of Milan, and generally resides here, received me at the terminus. The temperature was very hot; hotter than it is at Tehran. The crowds of spectators were immense, the women being particularly beautiful. The palace to which the Prince conducted me is most sumptuous, having been long built, but entirely restored by the first Napoleon when he conquered Italy and assigned this city to Prince Eugène as his Viceroy, a post he held for eight years. Later it was inhabited by Maximilian, brother of the present Emperor of Austria, and subsequently himself Emperor of Mexico, and there killed. He was Viceroy of this part of Italy for the Austrian Emperor until it was ceded to Italy, of which kingdom it is now an integral portion.

Opposite the palace is a church, the finest in Europe. As soon as I was a little rested, I went over to visit this fane. Being Sunday (27th July), it was full of men and women. To the right was a way leading by steps to the top. I accompanied the Prince to the summit by 570 steps, 200 being narrow, dark, and tortuous; then we reached terraces and extensive roofs, beyond which to the top the stairs are handsome. From the summit the Alps are seen, and Mount St. Bernard, by which the first Napoleon penetrated into Italy. The people in the streets appeared like pismires. The church is wholly built of white marble and is ornamented with 4,000 statues of marble or sculptures in high or low relief. It has been built by degrees, the work still going on; 500 years have elapsed since it was begun, another 100, it is said, must elapse ere it be completed. "Should a man come, suppose from America, on purpose, and were to look at nothing else but this one church and then return home, he would have no need to see any other work of art." We now returned home, dined at a great banquet with the Prince and notables, and then enjoyed from a window of the palace the spectacle of the illumination of the church from top to bottom with Bengal lights; at one moment all red, at another all blue, or green, or yellow, &c. The white pigeons that have their nests on all parts of this church, terrified with the strange splendour, took to flight, and in the darkness of the night flashed like lightnings with the effulgence. There must have been 20,000 people collected in the square to witness the sight.

Monday, July 28th.—Was reconducted by the Heir-Apparent and grandees to the station; took leave, and started for Saltzburg, in Austria. Passed by the Lake of Garda and the fortress of Peschiera to Verona, both of which fortresses fired salutes, and at the station of the latter I received the civil and military authorities. Thence, turning up the valley of the Adige, we reached Ala, the frontier station between Italy and Austria. Here the Italian officials in attendance on us took leave, and those sent by the Emperor of Austria to replace them were presented to us. Passing the strongly fortified post of Franzansvest, we arrived by sunset at a station where dinner had been prepared in a room for my suite. I received the authorities and inspected the troops, finding there a M. Gersisch, an artillery officer, who was formerly a professor in the College of Tehran, and two of whose best pupils are Muhammad-Hasan Khán, son of the Commander-in-chief, and Muhammad-Sádiq Khán, Qájár. His beard was grizzled somewhat, but he is strong and sound in health. Pursuing our journey, we could distinguish amidst the darkness of the night that we were keeping near the river and passing many ravines and bridges. Heavy rain came on with severe thunder and lightning. After supping, I fell asleep, and on awaking found we were at Innsbruck in a great crowd of officials and townspeople, who made a strange uproar. When left to myself I fell asleep again, awaking at day-dawn in another hubbub; and dozing off as soon as the train was anew in motion, awoke in about two hours. We were now in Bavaria. "Looking out at the country I saw a region like paradise. Enormous mountains clothed in forests of fir and pine; the plains all green and variegated with flowers of every colour. Though it was the very middle of summer, all seemed like the opening spring time; with numerous streams of water, all converging to the Danube. Harvest had not commenced; the air was cool like that of a summer station among the hills." We passed by Rosenheim, thence diverging to Frauenstein, passed the river Saltz, and entered Saltzburg, where the late Emperor Napoleon had had his meeting with the Emperor of Austria, and famous for its salt-mines. We were lodged in the ancient palace of the old bishops, who formerly held sovereign sway here. A mountain runs right into the town, and on it is a strong fortress, also built by the bishops.

Tuesday, July 29th.—Drove out to Schönbrun, viewed many of its curious old arrangements for the display of waterworks of various kinds, its rising crown, its pair of tortoises, its toy workshop, its *jets-d'eau* for ducking promenaders unawares, &c. Then hastened back to the station at Saltzburg for the train to Vienna. We passed through a beautiful and comparatively level country to Linz, being received at every station by the authorities. "The harvest was just cut, and the yellow shocks of corn standing in the midst of green fields formed a beautiful spectacle." Forests there were, and mountains in the distance. At Linz a breakfast had been prepared for me; I passed to it through crowds, the women being most beautiful. Austria is the country of all others that bears the bell for beauty and comeliness. A short distance beyond Hammelbach we came upon the Danube, skirted that noble stream for a time, and then again lost it, to reach St. Polten with its building-crowned hill. About sundown we reached Penzing, and at the station were met by His Majesty the Emperor, the Princes, and the Court, His Majesty having come some leagues from his capital to receive me with his interpreter Baron Schlechta, who speaks Persian fluently. On remounting, there were with His Majesty and myself in the carriage, my Grand-Vazīr, Mirzā Malkam Khān, Baron Schlechta, Count Dubcsky—Austrian Minister at Tehran, and Count Grenneville—in attendance on me. I am to lodge at Laxenburg, five leagues from Vienna, built by Maria Theresa; while His Majesty resides at Schönbrun, nearer to the capital. Arrived at Laxenburg, His Majesty formally presented to me the personages of his Court and family. His Heir-Apparent is a boy of about fourteen named Rudolf, a sweet youth. His Majesty then left, and on the following morning I went to Schönbrun to return his visit.

Thursday, July 31*st.*—Too hot to stir out. Dr. Polack, who was formerly Professor of Medicine at the College of Tehran, and for several years my physician, came to pay his respects, and I was very happy to see him. He is a handsome man, but has aged a little, and has married. In the evening drove about the park of the palace, and saw them feed the fishes in a lake with crumbs of bread; two hundred years they have bred in this lake (or pond), and are of a good size

There was a large lake also, with islands, on which I saw some wild geese. Had a row on the water, by the side of which is an old castle called the Knight's Castle, very much resembling the castles of demons or magicians of which one reads in story-books. I went all over it, and every room is fitted up in some curious or frightful manner. I also paid a visit to the Heir-Apparent.

Friday, August 1st.—Received visits from various German Princes living at or visiting Vienna—Count Andrassy, the Austrian Premier; (Sir A.) Buchanan, the English Ambassador; and Qabūli Pasha, the Ottoman Ambassador. In the evening went to Schönbrun to a state banquet given by the Emperor, who received me at the foot of the staircase. The second son of the King of Holland, Prince Alexander, who was one of the guests, kept us long waiting for him, so that we sat down late to table. His Majesty made excuses for the delay. The rooms and corridors of the palace of Schönbrun are very plain; its pictures and similar objects of art and luxury are few. The trees of its alleys in the garden are clipped with shears into the appearance of walls of verdure. Before leaving, I presented the Heir-

Apparent with the Order of my Portrait set with diamonds.

Saturday, August 2nd.—In the night it rained heavily, and the wind was very high. This cooled the air, and enabled me to go to Vienna and visit the Exhibition to-day—an instance of God's merciful providence; otherwise I doubt if I could have faced the excessive heat and the dust of the roads that had ruled hitherto. Having, therefore, offered up my thanks to God, I dressed, and then set out for the city with all my retinue. "On the road I observed many hares among the cultivated crops." As Vienna is in a hollow, nothing of it is seen until one is close upon it. For the same reason its climate in summer is very sultry and unwholesome. Its supply of water being bad, the Emperor is now bringing in a canal of pure water from springs in the snow-clad mountains some distance off. His Majesty met me at the station and accompanied me in a drive through the town, along a newly-constructed boulevard, past the Belvedere and the Arsenal, to the Exhibition, in the Imperial pavilion of which we breakfasted, and then entered the building itself. This is very large, and resembles an eastern bazaar, having in the centre a vast dome of great height, the whole of iron and glass. It is divided into sections, each occupied by the wares of one country. That of France was extensive, and I observed even specimens of the trunks of her trees, and of the leaves thereof, of her domestic and wild beasts and birds, let alone samples of silks, woollens, glass, arms, &c. The sections were large or small according to the importance of the country occupying each. Turkey, Egypt, Greece, Japan, and China were represented. I went through these with the Emperor, and so reached the Persian section. It was only three months before that orders had been issued for our merchants and others to send their wares; which was too late, and most of the things had not yet arrived. Still there were some fair contributions of choice articles. Here His Majesty left me, being desirous to go into the country on a visit to the Empress at her summer residence, she being in delicate health. I again made the tour of the sections, and met the Grand Duke Constantine, brother of the Emperor of Russia, whom I found pale and suffering. On inquiring his ailment, he told me that, in passing from one ship to another at Cronstadt, he had fallen and injured his foot. I afterwards inspected the architectural models erected outside the building, especially an Egyptian house and mosque, a Turkish house and coffee-shop, and a very pretty Persian edifice. This latter had been erected in a very short time by a Persian architect named Ismāʻīl, assisted by one Persian carpenter; he had managed in three months' time to acquire German fluently. The Austrian Government has expended seven crores on this Exhibition, of which it is hoped that one-half will be repaid by the entrance money of visitors, &c., and the other half will be lost, though more or less compensated in the gains of the people through the influx of foreigners and provincials.

The Emperor has been on the throne more than twenty-three years. His predecessor, who is still alive, abdicated; and now, seventy years old, lives at Prague. The Emperor's father, brother to the former Emperor, and still living, declined the crown, and now resides at Ischl during the summer, and passes the winter at Vienna.

Sunday was spent at home and I had a row on the lake with the Grand-Vazīr and Mīrzā Malkam Khān. On Monday I went for a day's shooting with the Emperor, which was conducted as follows: "We reached a place where a portion of a forest, two leagues in circuit, had been surrounded with a high screen of thick white linen, supported on wooden frames, not by ropes, thus preventing the escape of the game. We found His Majesty and the other sportsmen dressed as hunters, with a feather in his hat. At a certain distance apart, about 100 hiding-places had been constructed of planks, with a floor about two feet from the ground, and the outsides concealed with branches of fir and their leaves. In each were placed three or four breech loading rifles, with a supply of cartridges; and in each two or three grandees were seated, who were to shoot. I was shown to one at the head of the line, higher than the others. The Emperor occupied one lower down. I took the Emperor's guns placed there for me, and awaited the game, ready to fire. The Emperor's Grand Huntsman, a nobleman named Count Verbin, seventy years of age, deaf, and nearly blind, was there, and we conversed awhile about hunting in Persia and about the Emperor's hunting. The mode of the hunting was this. I have already mentioned that a very extensive screen had been set up. This screen was in suchwise that it came in front of us; there was also a screen behind us. From us, as we sat, to the screen in front of us was thirty feet. A door had been arranged in the screen some little distance further up than where I was posted, for the entry and exit of the game, and there was no other means to come or go. About forty or fifty men had collected the deer of the forest, and now drove them in through this door in packs of twenty or thirty head. These came on and passed the sportsmen at a distance of ten feet to receive their volley, and the sportsmen uninterruptedly fired at them with bullets; so that if they were not shot at one hiding-place they were at a second or third, and so on to the last, where there was no exit. These creatures ran about seeking an outlet and means of escape, but found none. They were all slain. So soon as not one of them was left breathing another batch was introduced, and were similarly slaughtered. I, too, fired a few shots. These animals are of the family of the stag, and are not very wild. Two or three batches were let in and killed. It was a beautiful hunt, and passed off pleasantly." I then returned to Schönbrun with the Emperor, drove in the park, which is open to the public, went into the Zoological Gardens at one end of it, and then returned home by train after dining. Before starting in the morning I had received the Corps Diplomatique of Vienna.

Tuesday, August 5th.—Had my photograph taken, then witnessed the application of a new pump that screws into the earth to a depth of ten cubits in ten minutes' time. It brought water to the surface from that depth, and is made of steel and iron. However hard the soil or rock may be, it bores them; it costs only 15 tūmāns (6*l.* 5*s.*) with all its apparatus. I ordered several sets to be brought to Persia.

In the afternoon went with my suite to Vienna to see the opera. The Emperor met me and took me to his box, where many of the Princes and Princesses, &c., were assembled. This theatre is the best in Vienna, if not the first in the whole world. The performances, dancing, and music were excellent. The dresses of the performers were continually changing, and always beautiful; with representations of enchantments, fairies, demons, &c. There was a moonlight scene of fairies in a wood, the moon being reflected in a river with waves. A fallen trunk of a tree served as a bridge, on which the fairies danced. Suddenly demons came forth and the fairies vanished. The demons danced. A genie then came and the demons fled; the fairies returned. The forest scene then changed to the polar regions, with glaciers and icebergs;

the snow fell, and the sea became covered with ice. On this white bears, seals, and walruses passed. A young prince was imprisoned in this wintry region, and was dying; when suddenly the nymphs of the North Pole and gnomes of the winter appeared, clad in white and with white hair. They produce fire out of the earth, warm the prince, and dance with him. He had been seized with his minister by the magician. At last there was a submarine scene, with all kinds of fishes and shells, corals, seaweeds, and zoophytes, springs gushing forth from the sea-bed, and sea-nymphs sleeping under these marine plants, each being a sly and saucy little child. Now a beautiful nymph would come forth from a shell or flower, and now an angel would descend from a cloud. They would dance, they would sink into the earth, they would ascend in balloons or on the backs of demons. "I had not dined, but still I wished it would not finish."

Wednesday, August 6th.—Received a visit from the Grand Duke Constantine, who was obliged to use a stick on account of his lameness. In the afternoon went to Schönbrun to review some troops with the Emperor. They were drawn up in five long lines like a column. We rode past each, and I particularly admired the Hungarian hussars.

The horses of Hungary being strong, the artillery is horsed from that country. It is said the Emperor wishes to change the Austrian white uniform for blue. There were about 15,000 troops present, of all arms. Among the spectators were some Arab chieftains from Algiers, dressed in their white cloaks and turbans, and on horseback. They had come to see the exhibition, and all spoke French well. The Emperor went and conversed with them. He and all his officers wore green feathers in their hats.

Thursday, August 7th.—Received the Emperor's brother Charles Louis, just come from his summer residence. About a fortnight ago he married his third wife, a princess of the House of Portugal, but born and grown up in Bavaria. In the evening visited Schönbrun, went up stairs with the Emperor, and was received on the landing by the Empress, who had come there on a visit, as had many other Austrian and German princes and princesses. These were one by one presented to me, the former by the Emperor, the latter by the Empress. "Her Majesty has lovely features, a graceful figure, is very kind, and an ornament to her station. She is rather delicate in health, and for this reason usually lives away from the capital. She is thirty-six years of age." We passed into a great hall where princes and princesses, Austrian or German, the Foreign Ministers, and others, were assembled; among them the Algerines of yesterday. Supper was served on small tables ranged around the hall; and after a little conversation, we took our seats at them. "At my table were seated the Empress, my Grand-Vazír, the Ottoman Ambassador Qabúli Pasha, Count Andrassy, and an elderly woman of distinction. Her Majesty expressed her regret that she had only been able thus to come in to bid me good-bye." After supper we went to another apartment to view some fireworks, among which the "Lion and Sun" were shown; also an engagement between a fort and a fleet. We then returned, the Empress taking my arm, while the Emperor gave his to "the elderly woman of distinction." At the foot of the staircase their Majesties took leave of me, and I returned home.

Friday, August 8th.—Having to return to Saltzburg to-day, I rose early, and very soon the Emperor, with his brothers, &c., his Ministers, &c., came to see me. I thanked His Majesty heartily for the pleasure I had derived from my transient visit to Laxenburg, and then the Count

Grenneville, in attendance on me, came to say it was time to start. "We rose; in another room I saluted the Austrian Ministry, but I did not say a last good-bye to them, nor to the Princes, as I imagined they would accompany me to the train. I drove to the station with the Emperor, and on alighting found they had remained behind. I was deeply grieved at thus missing the opportunity of bidding them adieu."

Taking again leave of His Majesty, I got into the train; but he remained standing until we left, and still saluted me as we glided away. At Lintz we breakfasted, as in coming. At Lambach the train stopped; and the King of Hanover, with his wife, daughter, and principal courtiers were on the platform waiting. I alighted, shook hands, and had a long conversation with His Majesty, whose summer residence is near that place. Hearing I was to pass, he had come on this visit expressly; but I was much grieved at seeing him. "He was a Sovereign, was esteemed, had his treasury and his army, and his crown. The Emperor of Germany wished to unite the whole of that country into one realm; and therefore it became necessary to take this King's territory out of his hands. War was declared;

and very soon was the King's army defeated, and his states incorporated with Prussia. The King fled with his family, and with his most valuable jewels; from that time to this he has resided in Austria. Besides these misfortunes, he has lost the sight of both his eyes, and his wife leads him about by the hand. He is very young, tall, and robust; but alas! he is blind. I was informed that he had one weak eye in his childhood; that he was playing with a purse of money, or something similar, and that this struck him in the sound eye and caused the blindness of both."

Leaving this station we reached Saltzburg at sundown, and were conveyed to the palace as on our former arrival. Qabūli Pasha, the Ottoman Ambassador at Vienna, has been instructed by his Government to accompany us to Brindisi.

Saturday, August 9th.—Leaving Saltzburg we journeyed through Bavaria to Kufstein, and there entered the Tyrol. On our road to Vienna we had passed this section by night, and had seen nothing of it. Now we witnessed its wondrous scenery, high mountains covered with forests, their skirts with cultivation, and dotted with villages. Near Innsbruck we had a severe storm of wind and rain, which cooled the weather.

In spite of this the crowds were great that stood to see our arrival. Troops were drawn out, with bands; and a salute of cannon was fired. The palace here, though somewhat simple, is very pretty and well kept; it contains, besides other pictures, portraits of the ancestry of the Emperor. The town is reached by a long viaduct which crosses the river, and is at least 2,000 cubits long. "These are the constructions that so much increase the costs and difficulties of making railways, since they must be very strong."

Sunday, August 10*th*.—Rain all night; still raining, with fog and clouds; but by degrees it cleared up. From Innsbruck, the road being on an ascent, the train went at a slow pace. The country all round was charming, and the rain had cooled the air; it was like paradise. We passed through ten short tunnels, and at length reached the summit of the Brenner Pass, at an elevation of 4,373 feet above the sea, with snowy peaks all around. Hence the streams flow to the north, by the Danube, into the Black Sea; or to the south, by the Po, into the Adriatic. At Schelleberg the road begins to descend, and the train having stopped, we got out to see the method used to prevent the carriages from rushing away. We walked as far as the village of Gossensasse, where I noticed two of my suite coming by themselves. On inquiry, they told me that, being Sunday, they had gone to see the village church, and had found it full of people. We, in fact, had walked through the village without seeing a single soul. They said: "The priest was in the pulpit delivering a sermon; when his eye alighted upon us, he became paralyzed in his pulpit, and bewildered with astonishment as to who we might be, with our caps and our costume, that had thus intruded into his church in this isolated mountain village."

"We went on a long way on foot, and after all did not see the train pass: so we had our pains for our trouble. It had passed us unobserved, and was waiting for us lower down." Mounting, we proceeded; the hills became gradually less lofty, the temperature rising in proportion. At Franzansvest we breakfasted, and thence reached Ala, the frontier of Italy, where our Austrian attendants took their leave, charged with a repetition of my warmest thanks to the Emperor for all his kindness and attentions. Although it was now night, we pushed on past Verona to Bologna. I had seen the country to the former, but missed that between the two cities. The night was clear, with bright moonlight. We got clear of the mountains and entered the plain. I supped in the train, and would not then lie down, as I promised myself a good rest and sleep at Bologna. All my companions slept; I continued gazing out on the country. The train was going twenty-five miles an hour. I noticed that the whole of the fields were of maize or rice, or mulberry trees for silk; and at day-dawn arrived at Bologna, stupefied with not having slept. "The authorities were at the station, also sleepless. Neither could they rightly attend to me, nor could I well make head or tail of them." On mounting a carriage a telegram arrived from the King, "who was at a hunting-station on the Alps," and expressed his pleasure at my again having entered his dominions. Went to a hotel selected for me by one of my attendants in advance; "but my apartment fronted the High Street of the town, and the noise of carriages, carts, waggons, shouts, and bands, was such that all hope of sleep was lost." I rested for a few hours, and esteemed even that a blessing.

In Vienna and Italy, &c., water-melons grow very fine, and much maize is raised; other fruits do not thrive well there.

Monday, August 11*th*.—Spent in seeing the city and neighbourhood of Bologna, with the old palace of the Popes; before leaving, on the Tuesday, I also visited the library and museum. We quitted this city about three hours to sunset, and I first saw the Adriatic in the neighbourhood of Rimini. We stopped at Ancona; but, being now dark, nothing of it was seen. Baron Final, the Italian Minister of Commerce and Agriculture, came and delivered to me a kind message from the King. Travelling all night we reached Brindisi on Wednesday. In this neighbourhood I remarked numerous plantations of ancient olive-trees and of cotton. On arriving at the station, Eshref Pasha, who was formerly the Ottoman Minister Resident at Tehran, Qabūlī Pasha—the Ottoman Ambassador to Vienna, Serkis Efendi—the Ottoman Minister resident in Italy, and others who had been sent from Constantinople to meet me, were presented by my Grand-Vazīr. Qabūlī Pasha took leave to return to Vienna. Next the Italian functionaries and foreign Consuls were presented. I then went on board the yacht of His Majesty the Sultan, named the "Sultāniyya," a more beautifully fitted yacht than any I had seen in Europe. There was also another Ottoman steamer for my suite. A high wind arising, some delay took place in shipping the baggage, &c., and we remained in port the remainder of the day, and all night. The latter part of our journey had been through a wild country, with willows and such like. "And now, thanks be to God that our trip through Europe has been performed in health and safety; may He further vouchsafe that what remains to be done will be equally auspicious and pleasant."

Thursday, August 14*th*.—Weighed anchor soon after dawn; but, before starting, the greater number of our suite came on board from the other steamer, complaining of its dirt and of the biting beasts with which it was infected, so that none had been able to sleep. The dinner and breakfast served up by the cook of His Majesty the Sultan was excellent. We passed by Otranto, the last we saw of Italy, and were off Corfu at sundown. This is the largest of the Seven Islands, which were formerly in the hands of the English, but were voluntarily ceded by them to Greece about ten years ago. At night the air was very clear, calm, and cloudless; the stars twinkled brilliantly, and the moon, which rose late, being twenty nights old, afforded me a charming spectacle as it came up out of the sea. I watched from the window of the ship the phosphorescence of the water in the foamy track of the paddle-wheels, rushing past like a white river. Amidst this incessantly did miniature flashes of lightning shine forth, as when a horse-shoe strikes fire on the road, or as a flint when struck with the steel. At dawn we were abreast of Cephalonia, and later we passed Zante, and then Navarino—where the united fleets of England, France, and Russia, destroyed and burnt those of Turkey and Egypt about forty years ago, thereby securing the independence of Greece. Steamers were not then general; all the fleets were sailing-ships. Seen through a telescope the hills of Greece are very sterile, destitute of water, and little inhabited. At sundown we rounded Cape Matapan, and there I saw some houses, each with a tower of great strength, as though these parts enjoy no security, and, therefore, each habitation is fortified by way of precaution. Not a stick grows on these arid mountains, which are all of rock. During the night we passed through the strait which separates Cerigo from the Morea and Cape St. Angelo. Soon after dawn on Saturday we were off the Gulf of Athens, and then passed the Island of Zea to our right, having Cape Colonna to our left. "This island is one of great celebrity, through the book written by Fenelon on the adventures of Ulysses, who was king of this island, was lost in the war of Troy, and whose son Telemachus went in search of him; but it is very small, barren, destitute of water, grass, and trees, as are the mountains of the mainland opposite to it." The ancient ruins on Cape Colonna, as seen at a distance through a telescope, resemble those of Persepolis in having many columns. We then passed between the islands of Andros and Negropont; and, so far, islands and main all belong to Greece.

An hour or so after sunset we were abreast of the little island of Psara, the first of those subject to Turkey, and behind which lies Scio, called by the Turks Saqiz (Mastic Island).

Sunday, August 17*th.*—As we passed the island of Tenedos on our right, early in the morning, a salute was fired from the castle, and after an interval we reached the entrance to the channel of the Dardanelles, along which many forts and batteries are planted. "They are all ancient, the Ottoman Sovereigns having merely repaired them, and have made nothing new." They all fired salutes; and at length we reached the town of the Dardanelles, where a large Ottoman man-of-war was anchored, and also fired a salute. Here we anchored for a time, so as to reach Constantinople at a convenient hour to-morrow morning. The Ottoman Grand-Vazīr, who had been sent by the Sultan to receive me here, came off from the town in a boat, as did also the Persian Envoy resident at Constantinople. I received the Grand-Vazīr in private audience first, and then he introduced and presented the officers of his suite and of the forts and province.

About an hour and a half before sundown we again weighed anchor and proceeded up channel towards the sea of Marmara. Our Grand-Vazīr went to return the visit of the Ottoman Premier in his ship, which followed in our wake as well as our former consort.

Monday, August 18th.—Arriving off Constantinople at a pre-arranged hour of the morning, my ship was stopped and the Ottoman Grand-Vazīr came on board to invite me to another of the Sultan's yachts, the "Pertev-i-Piyāla" ("Ray of the Goblet"), named after the Sultan's mother, and which had come out to meet me for that purpose. It was a smaller vessel than the

"Sultāniyya," but most beautifully fitted up, and the cabin of inlaid work. I went upon deck. Of the Persians resident in Constantinople about 3,000 came out in five very large steamers to meet us, and brought their ships very close to the "Pertev." Just then my Grand-Vazīr and suite were coming in boats to join me in her, and barely escaped being run down by one of those ships. As soon as they were safely on board we proceeded towards the entrance of the Bosphorus, having the Princes' Islands on our right. Nearing the city a steamer approached us with the foreign Ambassadors, &c., on board. We passed the ancient fortress of the Seven Towers—where former Sultans used occasionally to imprison European Ambassadors and even put them to death, the sea-wall of the city, and Seraglio Point with its ancient palace and inclosing walls. Advancing still, we passed Galata and Pera—the Frank quarters, and reached the Sultan's palace of Dolma-Bāgcha—called also the Palace of Beshik-Tash, the Imperial residence, built by the late Sultan 'Abdu-'l-Mejīd, brother of the reigning Sovereign. Passing this also we reached the Palace of Chirāgān, and thence crossed over to the Palace of Beyler-Beyi, on the Asiatic shore of the Bosphorus, our assigned residence, and so called from being built in the village of that name. Here His Majesty came on board to welcome us and conduct us ashore; he showed me over the palace and took his leave. He is about forty-four years old,—our own age. On our passage up the Bosphorus the forts and ships of war, several being ironclads, fired salutes. Shortly after, we went to the Palace of Dolma-Bāgcha to return His Majesty's visit; he received me most warmly at the foot of the staircase, took my hand, and conducted me to an upper chamber, where we conversed for a time. I then returned to Beyler-Beyi, inspected the details of its beautiful interior, took a bath, then walked in the hanging gardens with their marble steps, gaslights, ivy-clad supporting walls, fountains, statues in marble and bronze, stables of choice horses, pavilions, dove-cotes and doves, parrots, trained dogs and stud of hunters, poultry, and other animals of many kinds, all beautifully kept, and of which the Sultan is very fond. Thence returned home. The Golden Horn, an arm of the sea that separates Constantinople proper from Galata and Qāsim-Pasha, terminating among hills, and spanned by two bridges, is much narrower than the Bosphorus.

Tuesday, August 19*th.*—Received a message of congratulation and welcome from the Sultan's mother, through Ferīd Pasha. Afterwards gave audience to the Ottoman Ministry and dignitaries; then to the foreign Ambassadors, &c., accredited to the Sultan. Later made a tour up the Bosphorus as far as Biyuk-Dera, taking note of the different palaces and principal summer residences that adorn its shores; on my return went ashore at the pavillion of Gyuk-Sū, built by the late Sultan, and examined in detail all its pretty apartments and grounds.

On Wednesday breakfasted with His Majesty at the palace of Chirāgān, being received on the steps by the Sultan, surrounded by his principal Ministers. After an audience, at which only my Grand-Vazīr was present, His Majesty conducted me to another chamber, to a table laid out as in Europe. This day I had received a telegram from the Queen of England from Scotland, inquiring after my health, and containing a kind message for the Sultan also, which I now had the pleasure to communicate to His Majesty as we breakfasted together. We took coffee in another room, and I then returned home. In the afternoon drove out from the back gate of the palace to the summit of

Mount Chamlija, the highest behind Scutari, to enjoy the prospect, which was very beautiful, from the Black Sea to the Sea of Marmara, the Bosphorus, the cities and villages, and the islands. Inland, to the south, the signs of inhabitants were next to none. Returned home by a different road, over streets paved with stones, on which the horses had difficulty in keeping their feet.

On Thursday, after breakfasting at home, went to Constantinople to visit the mosque of Saint Sophia and the residence of the Persian Minister. But before starting I had a visit from the Sultan's eldest son, Prince Yusuf 'Izzu-'d-Dīn, who is fifteen years of age and of comely aspect. I conferred upon him the "Most Sacred" Order, with its ribbon, which is one of the great Orders of the Persian monarchy. On my way to Constantinople, I called at the palace of Chirāgān and returned the Prince's visit. Arrived at the landing-place of the city, I was received by the Governor, Ismā'īl Pasha, and conducted through crowds of Persians, Europeans, &c., by carriageable streets to the great mosque, where Kemāl Pasha, the Minister of Pious Foundations received me. The building was erected 1,310 years ago. It was first a pagan idol-temple, then a Christian church, and since the conquest of the city by Sultan Muhammed II, it has been a mosque. "Through lapse of time this structure has lost its original beauty; in one part there is a subsidence, with fissures. It resembles an old tree, the pristine vigour of which has departed." Performed my midday and afternoon service of worship here; visited the library, the upper galleries, and then proceeded to the Persian Mission, built by my Grand-Vazīr himself. Thence went home, and afterwards set out in state, with all my suite, to a great banquet given by the Sultan at the palace of Beshik-Tash, and to which the Ottoman and foreign Ministers were also invited. His Majesty received me at the foot of the staircase, conducted me first to a private apartment with my Grand-Vazīr, and then to a saloon where the foreign Representatives were drawn up in order. His Majesty spoke a few words to each, his foreign Minister, Rāshid Pasha, interpreting for him. I did the same, my Grand-Vazīr interpreting, "though I did not so much want his services, as I myself spoke in French." This occupied half-an-hour. Afterwards we went down stairs to a large and magnificent saloon, where the table was set out. I and the Sultan were at the head of the table; I on the right hand, the Sultan on the left. Far away below us were seated to the right, first, the Russian and English Ambassadors, two of my suite, Midhat Pasha, another of my suite, and so on to the bottom; and to the left, far below the Sultan, the Grand-Vazīr of Persia, the Grand-Vazīr of Turkey, two of my suite, the Ser-'Asker Pasha, &c., to the end." Large chandeliers, lighted with gas, shed splendour on the board. A gallery filled with musicians performed during the repast; "but when they struck up, our ears were filled, and it was impossible for any one to converse." It was a splendid banquet; and when over, His Majesty retired with me to a private room, where only the two Grand-Vazīrs, the Ser-'Asker, and the Russian and English Ambassadors were invited, and where coffee was served. After some little conversation I returned home; but the night was dark, and the passage by boat required caution.

Friday, August 22nd.—Received the Spanish Chargé d'Affaires, then an Armenian deputation, next two chief men of the Jews, dressed as Europeans, who read a long address in French; and, lastly, the photographer 'Abdu-'l-'lāh, a French Christian who has assumed this name, and is very clever at his art. He took several negatives of my person in my state dress. Afterwards, mounting my qāyiq, I paid a visit to the "'Azīziyya" ship of war, built in London. Exercises were gone through, and all was in excellent order. I then went to the "Pertev" yacht for an excursion to the Princes' Islands, and salutes were fired by all the fleet. I visited each of the islands, on one of which is the Naval College, with a training ship attached, the others being inhabited by private persons. Returning, we hugged the shore of Asia, passed several villages with extensive vineyards of excellent grapes, and so on by Scutari to our palace.

On Saturday the Sultan took me a drive into the country to breakfast with him at his mother's country seat. Returning, he accompanied me up stairs, remained some time with the two Grand-Vazīrs present, testified profound friendship, and then left. I escorted him to the foot of the staircase.

There are several large steamers that ply on the Bosphorus, carrying passengers from place to place. They chiefly belong to foreigners, and have a space partitioned off for women. They are a source of great danger to boats, and accidents frequently happen. "The boatmen never give notice of these, lest it should spoil their trade."

Last evening I had sat down to dinner, when

repeated cannon-shots being fired caused me some alarm. On looking out of a window I saw sparks of fire, and knew that a conflagration had broken out; in the morning I learnt that 800 houses had been consumed in Qāsim-Pasha.

This afternoon I went to the gardens of the palace of Chirāgān, where the Sultan keeps some wild beasts. There were many peacocks. Among the tigers was one in a great fury; he roared continually, and faced the spectators. I had not seen one like him in any of the collections of Europe. Another tiger, such as I had not seen before, was marked as usual with stripes, but had besides on his back and flanks a number of white spots like those of the young red deer. Afterwards I went over the palace itself, and especially admired the bath. The baths of Turkey are not like those of Persia, built away from the house and with a tank in the middle (where all get in together and all wash together). On the contrary, they are within the house, on the same level with the apartments, have marble basins around them with taps for hot and cold water. The bath is warmed from beneath by flues, the furnace of which is fed from without. Although it was now dark, I was shown all over the palace, the ladies' apartments, their garden, those of the

Sultan's mother, &c., and I found them all beautifully furnished. Large sums must have been expended here from first to last. Serkis Efendi, the architect who has erected the present structure, speaks French well. I then returned home and dined, after which an ugly-looking French-speaking conjuror amused us with some surprising feats of legerdemain.

First, he drew out of his breast a thin piece of wood without a hole in it. On this he laid his hand and produced a live canary bird, which he allowed to fly away, and which went and perched at a distance. He then took a ruby ring from the finger of one of my princes and placed it on a table with two lemons. He asked us to choose either of these. This was done, and he cut the other in two, to show that it contained only its natural strata of parts. He next took up the ring and made it disappear. He then went and brought back the canary, held it in his hands, and made it disappear also. Now cutting in two the selected lemon, he produced from it the canary, with the prince's ring firmly bound to one of its legs with a red silken riband.

He next took my Grand-Vazir's pocket-handkerchief,—marked by himself with his name in the corner, and held it while one of my princes cut it in two. He made it into a ball, rammed it into a pistol, and fired it away. He then placed a wine-bottle on the table, took another handkerchief from another of the company, cut it in two likewise, and made one of the princes set fire to it. This he rubbed in his hand and made it vanish. He next asked for four cigar-cases, which were furnished by members of our party. These he placed on the table and begged that one might be selected. This was done by the Grand-Vazír, who gave it to one of the princes to hold. He then took an axe and smashed the bottle, out of which came a live dove having the Vazír's handkerchief bound round its foot, with his name marked upon it. And finally he drew forth from the cigar-case in the prince's hand, whole and uninjured, the other handkerchief which had been cut and set fire to.

Again, he took three rings from different people's fingers and gave them to another to hold. He next took a wine-glass, and into it he broke an egg, yolk and white, adding thereto the three rings. He then took Dr. (Sir Joseph) Dickson's hat, and into it poured the contents of the vessel, yolk, white of egg, and rings. Turning the hat, now, upside down, the three rings came forth, each tied to a nosegay, while the hat was found to be unsoiled.

He took another ring from one of the princes and placed it on the table with two water-melons, one of which was selected and the ring made to disappear. The selected melon was cut open, and out of it came a fresh hen's-egg. This was broken, and in it was found a whole walnut, which he placed before me on the ground, gave a hammer to one of the princes, and upon his cracking the walnut therewith, the ring was discovered inside it. Many other curious feats also did he perform.

The following day was chiefly spent at home, where I gave audience to the Ottoman President of the Privy Council, and to the Minister of Foreign Affairs. I then paid a visit to the Ottoman Grand-Vazīr at his waterside residence; went again as far as Biyuk-Dera, and returned home.

Monday, August 25th.—Went to the palace of Dolma-Bāgcha to take leave of the Sultan, and met with the same honours and ceremonies as on my arrival. On returning home, the English Ambassador had an audience, and shortly after the Sultan returned my visit of adieu. His Majesty conducted me in his own canopied state barge to the "Sultāniyya," the steamer in which I had come from Brindisi, and which, to say the truth, is a splendid ship. When His Majesty at length left me, I accompanied him to the foot of the accommodation ladder, and all the ships of war fired a salute. At about two hours and a half to sunset we weighed and I bid adieu to Stāmbūl. On nearing Therapia and Biyuk-Dera, the men-of-war on station and attendance on the foreign Ambassadors came in sight. Those of the English and Russian representatives are very large and beautiful, with numerous crews, who manned the yards and cheered. My ship stopped, and the Russian Ambassador came in his boat on board and had an audience. Our Ministers Resident in London and Constantinople, with Narīmān Khān and Mr. Thomson, who had accompanied me everywhere throughout my tour, went ashore with the Russian Ambassador. On our passing the forts at the entrance of the Black Sea, they all fired salutes. We saw the new moon of the month Rajab set in the sea, and as the weather was calm we were not incommoded. May the gratulations of God and His salutation and peace be upon 'Alī, son of Abu-Tālib, the Prince of all those of the Faith! This evening poor Eshref Pasha, the Ottoman Court official in attendance upon us, fell down twenty steps of the ship's ladder and broke an arm, besides hurting his head. Dr. Tholozan and others treated him medically. In the course of to-day, before leaving the palace, Dr. Tholozan presented to me Marco Pasha, the head physician to the Sultan, and we had a long conversation with him. He is a man of forty-five, thin, yellow faced, who shaves his beard and wears mustachios; he knows French well, is said to be of Greek origin, and has long been the Sultan's physician.

Tuesday was calm, and we saw many fishes as big as horses sporting round the ship. In the afternoon a light breeze from the north sprang up, and the ship pitched and rolled somewhat. We passed Sinope in the night, where the Russians burnt the Ottoman fleet in the Crimean war. Wednesday was equally calm. Little birds came flying to the ship, though no land was in sight. They were hungry and remained. They essay to return to the shore, but have not strength. One was caught and put in a cage; it drank some water, and soon after died. Towards sundown we again sighted land near Trebizond, the buildings of which I saw through a telescope. Again we left the shore, and after nightfall a storm of thunder and lightning, with black clouds, arose from the west and continued all night, but without wind.

On Thursday at dawn the storm increased in severity, and heavy rain fell. The electric fluid struck the sea not more than fifty feet from the ship, with an explosion like that of a thousand cannons. A few hours later we were near to Poti, our destined port. Thanks be to God that we have escaped the dangers of the high seas! Our large ship was obliged to anchor at a distance from the shore. Our consort, with my retinue, was already there, having made sail and taken a more direct inshore course than we had ventured upon. I returned thanks for their safety. A small steamer from Poti brought out Prince Menschikoff, my former Russian attendant, to receive me this time also. The sea being rough, there was no possibility to bring the little steamer alongside; first she damaged herself considerably, and then carried away the ladder of the "Sultāniyya." Upon this, patience for a while was had recourse to; and the sea subsiding somewhat the two ships were at length brought together. Some of the baggage, some of the princes, some of my servants, and I myself, got into the Russian vessel. I saw poor Eshref Pasha with his head bound up, his face black and blue, and his arm in a sling; I was much grieved for his mishap. I passed by a narrow plank from ship to ship; but most of my people remained behind, with the chief part of the luggage. In half an hour we entered the Rion, which has a few miserable huts on each bank, like those of the peasants of Māzandarān and Gilān. Its soil is marshy, its air unwholesome. Fever and ague are frequent there. It has no port, and large ships must lie in the offing. One English steamer and two Turkish sailing-vessels were there. The country is one tract of forest to the mountains, which are one mass of forest also.

On the river bank many flags were planted and a small room prepared. The Grand-Duke Michael, brother of the Emperor and Governor-General of the Caucasus, was at the landing-place to receive me. A crowd of many nationalities had also collected; Circassians, Lesghians, Armenians, Georgians, Muhammedans, Dāgistānīs, Open-Heads (Mingrelians; who wear no head-dress, like our Blue-Coat boys), Franks, &c. This place is part of the Open-Head country. So are its inhabitants called, and so do they go about; men, women, children, eternally follow the custom of wearing no cover for the head. The chief town of the Open-Heads is Kutais, which lies between Poti and Tiflis.

The Grand-Duke was not at St. Petersburgh during my visit, and I was therefore much pleased to meet him. He is the youngest of the Emperor's brothers. He wears whiskers on both cheeks, but shaves his chin. His eyes are blue and pleasing; he is tall of stature, and robustly stout. In half an hour's time we went to the station and started, the carriages of the train all having access to one another. The line has been newly made, and is single, the same rails being used by the trains in coming and going. The construction has been very difficult, as the whole of its course is through forest, morass, and water. To drain such land and construct a road is not easy. Where the morass ends, mountains begin. The line there becomes tortuous and up-hill, with many bridges. After reaching the summit-level it again descends to reach Tiflis. Our pace was necessarily slow, about two-and-a-half leagues per hour. The rain was falling heavily. In five hours we reached a station near Kutais at sundown, where we made a light dinner in a small room. A company of local troops was drawn up to receive us, dressed in the quaint ancient costume of the country, something like that of the French Zouaves and native levies of India, with open coats of red cloth, red turbans, a pistol and powder-horn in their belts; but they had needle-guns, made at Tula. We travelled all night, and reached Tiflis early in the morning, while the lamps were still burning in the streets. The grandees brought the usual bread and salt, with a long address written out in Persian.

The town of Tiflis consists of two parts, the old and the new, situated respectively on the two sides of a stream almost dry at this season, but crossed by a bridge which unites them. On a hill are the remains of an old castle. The new town is the quarter of the Francs, where are some wide, paved streets, schools, public edifices, and the residences of the Governor-General and Lieutenant-Governor. The peak of Mount Qāf (Kūh-i-Qāf), which the Franks have named Kazbek, is visible from the town. It is very high, and full of snow. The Russians have constructed a road over this chain, so that a carriage may pass to Vladi-Kafkas, which is on the road to Moscow and Astrakhan. The hills in the immediate neighbourhood are bare;

further off they are clothed with forest. The climate is bad; excessively hot in summer and autumn, but liable to interruptions of very cold winds and rain; so that fevers and agues abound. Its population is about 50,000, principally strangers —Persians, Georgians, Russians, Dāgistānīs, Circassians, Germans, Armenians. Water-melons, grapes, pears, and cucumbers of fine quality grow here. Paid visits to the Grand-Duke and Grand-Duchess, and received their visit in return. Drove out with him, and in the evening went to the theatre with them. It is very small and plain, capable of holding at the utmost 200 persons. The play was in Russian, and the Russian and Georgian national dances were danced,—the latter resembling those of Persia, and accompanied by the same kinds of instruments.

On my return home, received news of the ultimate safe landing at Poti of the remainder of my people and baggage, not without considerable damage to the Sultāniyya and to the small shore steamer, as the sea had continued to rise after my landing. It had been already arranged that we should all cross the Caucasus and go to Petrowski on the Caspian, there to embark on the steamer that was to convey us to Enzeli. But, as I dreaded a long and, perhaps, disagreeable voyage, this plan was altered so far as that I, with ten followers, should go to Baku, and the others, with the baggage, should embark at Petrowski, to call and pick me up at Baku.

On Saturday, Bahman Mirzā (the Shah's fugitive uncle) came in from Dāgistān with seven grown-up sons, and was admitted to an audience. In the evening, dined at a great banquet given by the Grand Duke, at which Bahman Mirzā was also present. It was followed by an illumination and fireworks; also by a cossack dance, in which pistols are fired. Received a telegram from the Emperor making kind enquiries; also another from Tehran, informing me of the death of a certain holy man who was on his way to the sacred shrines of Kerbela, &c., but who breathed his last at Kirind. This intelligence grieved me much. An envoy also came from the Patriarch of Etchmiazin with an address.

Sunday, August 31st.—The princes, &c., left Tiflis for Petrowski in the morning. Later in the day I too started for Baku. Five carriages were prepared for me, each with many horses. Drove through old Tiflis, with its intense heat and stifling dust. Once outside the town, not a vestige of human habitation or industry was visible as far as the eye could reach; only that every two leagues we came to a post-house, where horses are changed. For about six leagues from Tiflis, sand had been spread on the road, which somewhat kept down the dust; beyond that distance it was frightful. Dined, and afterwards slept, at two different stations; and travelling all day on Monday, reached Ganja (Elizabethpol) before sundown, being escorted and met by Cossacks everywhere. Here the Governor came out a distance to meet me, and lodged me in his very poor residence. In these regions the women, and even the children, carry arms.

Tuesday, September 2nd. — Left Ganja and reached the bank of the Kur at Mangi-chāwur, where I found a felt tent pitched for me, and a hut of boughs and grass erected for the Grand-Vazīr; the first as hot as a bath, the latter airy, but filled with people. On the road, the carriage containing my jewels broke down, and caused a considerable delay. Before they came up, I breakfasted off a large fish, fresh caught in the river with a net. To ferry us over, two barges were fastened side by side, planks were laid across them, a few things were put away in their holds, the rest and ourselves occupied the deck. A rope was fastened to a tall mast, and by this the apparatus was pulled from shore to shore. Our carriages went over first, next I, then the Grand-Vazīr, &c., with the baggage. After we had again started, I shot from the carriage, as we travelled along at post haste, several of the birds we call in Persian " green jackets." About two hours after sunset we reached the Turyān-Chāyi (R. Turyan),—the first place where I saw any cultivation since leaving Tiflis. Here some of the chief people from the town of Sheki (Nukhi, in Dāgistān) had come to receive me. The post-house was so full of mosquitoes that I caused a felt tent to be erected, and slept out in the air.

Wednesday, September 3rd.—The magnates of Ganja and Sheki took leave. Started on our journey, saw some villages and gardens irrigated from the Turyān, and reached Gok-Chāy (Blue River), where we were met by the Governor of Baku and Shīrwān, whose jurisdiction extends thus far. Many of the magnates and learned Muslins of Shīrwān had also come. After receiving them and changing horses, we continued our course, noticing many villages watered by the Gok. This plain is fertile, but is very sultry. Passing by some other streams and villages, all watered from the Dāgistān mountains, we arrived at Aq-Sū (White Water), a large village, with extensive gardens and orchards producing beautiful fruit. It put me in mind of a certain village near Tehran, but this latter is larger and in better condition. There are many fruiterer's shops in this place. I walked about, ate some fruit, performed my devotions, and then started again. We had to ascend the valley of the Aq-Sū by a winding road on the side to our right, crossed a ridge, and at length reached Shamakhi two hours after sunset. The town was illuminated everywhere, and the inhabitants testified the utmost joy at my arrival. I was taken to the house of a certain Armenian named Lalaieff, which was formerly the residence of the Governor, and overlooks the whole town. This was greatly damaged a few years ago by a severe earthquake, which frequently happen.

Thursday, September 4th.—Travelled over a dry and wretched country all day, and arrived near Baku at the post-house of Sarāyī before dark, where the Governor met me with all his officers, military and civil. We reached Baku itself two hours after sunset, and I found that my suite were just arrived before me in the Constantine steamer. By way of illumination, all the naphtha springs of the region had been set fire to. With this and the moonlight, I was able to see that a number of very good houses in European style have been built here facing the sea, where the Governor's house is also, to which I was taken. I gave audience to a large company of the notables, dined, and four hours after sunset embarked. The port has this singularity, that large ships can come and lie alongside the shore. A thousand thanks did I offer to God Most High that once more I was safe on board this ship. Prince Menschikoff and the other official attendants, &c., were with me, and another steamer had the remainder of my suite on board. The wind was calm, and I slept in comfort. The districts of Sheki and Shirwan produce good camels. The carts are there drawn by buffaloes, &c., but the wheels are of wood only, without iron.

Friday, September 5th.—The sea is calm, we are nearing Enzeli. Dressed in state ready to disembark. But, by degrees, the sky became overcast from the south and west. With a telescope I could see a large Russian man-of-war steamer, anchored at Enzeli and awaiting my arrival, pitching and rolling fearfully; as was also a sailing merchantman. There being no alternative, we made all speed, reached the anchorage, and with the greatest difficulty the man-of-war fired a few guns. I could see my turret at Enzeli, and the people on the shore; but our vessel could go no nearer. It was a matter of necessity that shore-boats and my little steamer should come out to land us; but with this burst of bad weather it was impossible. When I could no longer remain on the deck I went below, undressed in despair, sat down, and resigned myself to the will of God. My suite also took off their uniforms and decorations, varying this operation with vomitings. Each one slunk into a corner, as none could stand up. It wanted but two hours to sunset; the rain was pouring in torrents, and the sea was so tumultuous that it was not possible to look out. The mast-heads touched the waves to the right and left as the ship rolled. The sea made a clean breach over us, and the ship listed so much that nothing remained but for her to upset, and for us to be rolled into the sea. The cabin furniture was dashed about; the creakings and dashings were frightful, and we feared the ship would break up. Rain was falling over head; the waves were boiling beneath us; the ship was full of water; no one could walk for her violent motions; besides which, the planks of the deck were so wet that one's feet could not retain a hold of them. I was oppressed with the thoughts that when, after my tour through Europe, my own home at Enzeli was in sight, and when so many of my servants had assembled there to welcome me, such a misfortune had befallen me, and that, should this storm last three days we should inevitably drag our anchor and be carried out to sea. These impressions made life a burden indescribable; I felt somewhat unwell; I perspired incessantly from the heat and from apprehension; the wind struck to my chest, and I coughed. I could not sleep by day or by night.

Saturday, September 6th.—The sea, rain, and wind are tempestuous as ever, perhaps worse. Our consort, with the princes, &c., came in and anchored. And so things went on all day. I slept a couple of hours. Suddenly I heard voices. They told me a shore-boat had come alongside. I rose and saw that a boat with a crew of twelve men had come at the risk of their own lives to enquire news of me, and that the sea was abating. A written answer was sent ashore by the boat. Again an interval occurred, and dawn of the 7th was at hand, when a second boat came alongside, into which two of my suite threw themselves and departed. Morn appeared; other boats came off; some went away in them. The weather became promising, and at length my little steamer was seen to be approaching out of the back-water lagoon. When she was alongside, it was no easy matter to get from one vessel to the other, as they kept at a certain distance; so they brought my barge alongside, into which I got, somehow or other, reached my steamer, and was pulled up on to her deck by hand. I thanked God. I breathed freely again. We reached the landing-place of Enzeli. I went to my house and held an audience for those who had come from Resht and Tehran. Again I returned thanks. At night there was a grand display of fireworks, after which I went to bed and slept in peace.

www.ingramcontent.com/pod-product-compliance
Lightning Source LLC
Chambersburg PA
CBHW020918230426
43666CB00008B/1483